The Christian & Witchcraft

Dealing with Demonic, Satanic, and Occultic Darkness Through the Power of God

Charlie Avila

The material in this book was first taught through Sunday messages at Clovis Christian Center and presented on the teacherofthebible.com website in the United States.

Clovis Christian Center
3606 N. Fowler Ave
Fresno, California, USA 93727-1124

ISBN: **9781691502523**
(Softcover Edition)

Printed in the United States

CONTENTS

DEDICATION

This book is affectionately dedicated to Clay and Roberta Rooks. They are faithful servants of the Lord who work behind the scenes to get things done for the Lord and His kingdom. They are especially good at prayer, intercession, and encouragement. And they understand the spiritual warfare associated with the subject of this book. Thank you for your love and devoted service.

PREFACE

The subject of witchcraft is very disturbing and ugly. It conjures up thoughts of witches flying on brooms and people in dark coats mixing up some magic potion in an old laboratory. Many well-meaning people relegate witchcraft to some remote African village controlled by witch doctors or sorceresses.

As Christian believers, we need to understand that many cultures and nations are dominated by witchcraft and idolatry. Moreover, the Bible says a lot about witchcraft. As a Pastor, I have dealt regularly with people who are involved with perverse things associated with satanic darkness. Many of the stories are found in the following chapters.

This book is divided into two sections: Witchcraft in the New Testament and Witchcraft in the Old Testament. The chapters under each section alternate between dealing with the biblical text where God's people had to confront witchcraft, and personal encounters that I've had with people involved with witchcraft in everyday life. I believe this combination of theological study and practical application gives the reader powerful and confirming truths that will establish him in the faith.

I have presented the chapters in a systematic order where one truth builds on another, so I ask that you read from the beginning straight through to the end. Most chapters are short and get right to the point of the teaching. The personal stories provide sufficient detail to give the reader a good understanding of the circumstances involved with each encounter. This detail is deliberate and intentional. Many Christians are completely unaware that certain objects, books, symbols, and paraphernalia involve witchcraft or satanic associations.

May the Lord give you discernment, insight, and understanding as you study this very important subject. As Paul prayed in Ephesians 1:17-18, "That the God of our Lord

Jesus Christ, the Father of glory, may give to you the spirit of wisdom and revelation in the knowledge of Him, the eyes of your understanding being enlightened." May the Lord open our spiritual eyes to see.

Jesus Christ is Lord. To God be the glory.
Charlie Avila, February 2020

Witchcraft in the New Testament

I am amazed at how often God's people in the Bible had to confront witchcraft.

Moses and Aaron confronted the "wise men, sorcerers, and magicians"[1] of Egypt in Pharaoh's court in Exodus 7-10; "Balaam the soothsayer"[2] was hired to curse Israel, but later seduced them sexually in Numbers 22-25; King Saul foolishly consulted "a witch at Endor" in 1 Samuel 28; the prophet Daniel dealt with "magicians, astrologers, sorcerers, and Chaldeans" in Babylon in Daniel 1-5; both King Ahaz and King Manasseh "practiced soothsaying, used witchcraft, and consulted spiritists and mediums."

The Old Testament (OT) uses sixteen different Hebrew words for "wizards," "mediums," "spiritists," "psychics," "necromancers," "sorcerers," "enchanters," "witches," "soothsayers," "diviners," "magicians,"

---

[1] We know from 2 Timothy 3:8 that at least two of them were named "Jannes and Jambres," and these men "resisted Moses," "resisted the truth" and were of "corrupt minds."

[2] See Joshua 13:22. Balaam was from the city of "Pethor." Pethor means "soothsayer" according to the Brown-Drivers-Briggs Hebrew Dictionary. He was later killed by the sword in Numbers 31:8.

"astrologers," "observer of times," and those with "familiar spirits." The New Testament (NT) has nine similar words. The Bible says a lot about these servants of Satan.

However, make no mistake about it – *God really hates witchcraft.* He detests it because He knows how it will destroy our lives. The Lord calls witchcraft "an abomination," "rebellion," "evil," and a "work of the flesh."[3] The prophet Samuel made the famous declaration that "rebellion is as the sin of witchcraft." It really "provokes the Lord to anger." Under OT law, anyone who was a witch, sorceress, medium, or spiritist was not permitted to live – "they shall surely be put to death; you shall stone them with stones."[4] God Himself said, "I will set My face against that person and cut him off from his people" because he has "prostituted" and "defiled" himself.[5] In the NT, "sorcerers" will be thrown into "the lake of fire" because they have "deceived all the nations" and "not repented of their sorceries."[6] Again, God's Word says a lot about this subject.

In this first section, I want to look closely at the four instances in the Book of Acts where the early apostles confronted witchcraft in various forms. It may startle Christians to know that the apostle Peter had to rebuke "Simon the sorcerer" in Acts 8; the apostle Paul brought judgment upon "Elymas the sorcerer" in Acts 13; Paul and Silas confronted a "slave girl with a spirit of divination" in Acts 16; and, when a revival broke out in Acts 19, the new believers in Ephesus "burned scrolls of sorcery and magic."[7]

Also, I will share some personal stories of how I've had to deal with witchcraft in my pastoral ministry over the years. I believe these testimonies will reveal key aspects of

---

[3] See Deuteronomy 18:12, 1 Samuel 15:23, 2 Kings 17:17, and Galatians 5:19-20.
[4] See Leviticus 20:27 and Exodus 22:18.
[5] See Leviticus 19:31 and 20:7.
[6] See Revelation 9:21, 18:23, 21:8, and 22:15.
[7] See Acts 8:9-24, 13:6-12, 16:16-24, and 19:17-20.

witchcraft that Christian believers are facing today. The evil is the same, but the tools and methods are sometimes different. The bondage never changes, however.

Let's begin with a nurse that I met here in my hometown.

THE CHRISTIAN & WITCHCRAFT

1

Rosie the Spiritual Guide

The elderly African-American woman was completely perplexed. She was frustrated and desperate. Her beautiful daughter, Tamika,[8] was in her late twenties, had a Master's Degree in Nursing from one of the top universities in California, and worked as a registered nurse at one of the best hospitals in this area. She was a beautiful young lady with a good personality, so why could she not find or keep a boyfriend?

Some strange things began to happen. Good-looking, well-educated men were asking her out on dates, but no one ever came back a second time. In fact, there were times when the dinner dates lasted less than one hour. The man would pick up Tamika at 6:00 p.m., and by 7:00 p.m., she was being dropped off. The man was never seen again.

This really bothered the mother. Somehow, she obtained the phone number of the last guy who dated her. She was very curious. She called him to ask some questions.

---

[8] The names in this story have been changed to keep confidentiality. The story, of course, is true.

"I see that you picked up my daughter on Saturday evening for dinner, but you were already back in the driveway within one hour? Did something go wrong?"

"Yes," the man said right away. "Ma'am, I don't know how to say this to you, and I don't mean to disrespect you or your daughter, but she is very weird. Something is really wrong with her."

"What do you mean?" the mother asked.

"Well, shortly after getting in my car, she suddenly became very angry. In fact, she attacked me while I was driving the car. She has really long fingernails, and she began clawing at my face, hands, and arms. Rather than get physical and possibly hurt her in defending myself, I turned right around and dropped her off. That was my first and last date with her. I'm sorry, ma'am."

The mother was completely incredulous. How could this be? What had happened to her daughter? She never saw any of this behavior at home. She worried that Tamika may have an undiagnosed mental condition or perhaps she was depressed. Maybe she was tormented by an evil spirit. Her mind was racing with many thoughts.

The mother had been raised in a Christian home and had attended churches all her life. She began to cry out in desperation to the Lord.

"Lord, what do I do? Where can I go to get help for Tamika? How do I even talk to her about this issue? Is there anyone that can help me?"

One day she was driving down Fowler Avenue. As she drove by a church, she saw the church sign with the name of the church, the Pastor's name, church phone number, and a list of various service times. As she looked at the phone number, she heard in her heart, "Call that number and talk to that Pastor."

She had already passed the church, so now she had to loop back and write down the name and number she saw on the sign. She wrote down: "Pastor Charlie Avila, 559-

291-2595." When she got home, she immediately called the number and left a message on the answering machine.

I got to the church office the next day and heard the message – "Hello, my name is Chloe Johnson. I'm having a problem with something very important. Can the Pastor please call me? I got your name and number off of the sign in front of the church. Thank you." She left her number and I called within a few minutes.

I made arrangements to go to her house. I realized that she lived in the far northern outskirts of Fresno in a ranch style home with about two acres of property. She told me that she was 67 years old and her health was quite poor. She looked frail and tired. But she got right to the point of my visit.

She told me about Tamika's dates, and especially about what happened with the last man who picked her up. Then she added this important piece of information: "I did notice that some strange things have been happening with her since she went up to the Bay Area, near San Francisco. She told me that she went to seek some spiritual advice from some kind of guide or counselor. The lady she saw apparently gave her some roses that she keeps in her closet."

To make a long story short, Tamika had visited a psychic in San Francisco. She knew the area well because that's where she had gone to graduate school and she had some old friends there.

I asked the mother, "Do you think that Tamika would be willing to meet with me? Can I come back at a time when she is at home and we can talk about these things?"

Within one week, I made an appointment to meet with Tamika. As a precaution, I recruited one of the elderly prayer warriors (intercessors), Ann, from our church to go with me. We prayed and fasted before we went.

When Ann and I walked into the house and met Tamika, she was wearing a light-blue nursing uniform. It appeared she had just gotten off of work. We met in the family room with the mother.

This was a very sensitive subject because I didn't know how much the mother told Tamika about why she contacted me. Anyway, the Holy Spirit was definitely leading me as I asked her a lot of questions. Tamika was very friendly and answered everything right away.

Somehow, we got on the subject of the visit to the psychic. She was surprisingly candid and spoke about it as if it was a normal relationship.

"Yes, I visited a psychic in the Bay Area. I was battling a lot of negative things in my life, including depression, and I needed some answers."

I was hoping that she would bring up the issue of the roses that she had in her closet, but she didn't.

I asked, "What was the final outcome of your visit? Did you get any help or advice? Have you seen any changes for the better?" I asked these questions knowing fully the terrible consequences of visiting a sorceress. Witchcraft always brings curses into people's lives.

It was at this point that she said, "Well, she did give me some roses. I have them in my closet. The psychic told me that I can use these roses to talk to my personal spirit guide. The name of this spiritual guide is Rosie. I suppose that's why she gave me the roses. It's my point of contact to speak with Rosie. I talk to Rosie in my room every day."

I asked her, "Can we go into your bedroom? I want to see these roses."

She immediately agreed.

She went straight to the closet, slid open the door, and pulled out three, long-stemmed, red roses. They were fake, but they looked real.

It was while she held these roses in her hands that I said, "Tamika, do you realize that you are dealing with something demonic? You're ensnared in witchcraft. You're not talking to just anyone named Rosie; you're talking to an evil spirit. You're playing with fire. This is very dangerous for your personal life."

With that bold statement, I opened my Bible to Deuteronomy 7:25-26. I added, "Do you understand that many people bring cursed objects into their homes, little knowing that they bring curses into their lives? You've opened your spirit up to demons. A lot of potentially evil things are going to come into your life."

I was surprised that Tamika did not react negatively. She agreed that something was very wrong about these roses and talking to Rosie the spirit guide.

When she was in this agreeable frame of mind, I began to talk to her about Jesus Christ. I told her about salvation. I plainly stated that she needed to repent of this participation with witchcraft and she needed to renounce what she was doing.

"Tamika, you need to get rid of these roses and repent of this involvement with a psychic. The enemy has placed a hook in your life. You must cut yourself off completely from this and throw the roses away."

With the added prayers and counsel of Ann, the intercessor, we prayed for Tamika to receive the Lord into her life. She repented and renounced her involvement with witchcraft. She asked the Lord to forgive her of what she had done. We took the roses and cut them up and threw them in the trash. I prayed some closing prayers over her and her bedroom. We left with glad and sincere hearts.

I called the mother several times over the next few weeks, and apparently, everything was now going along fine. I encouraged both of them to get actively involved in a local church. They were welcome to come to our church. They did have relationships with some churches that were near their home. I praised the Lord for His work of deliverance in Tamika's life.

YouTube Video: **The Christian and Witchcraft 01**

2

Simon the Sorcerer
Acts 8:9-24

"But there was a certain man called Simon, who previously practiced sorcery in the city and astonished the people of Samaria, claiming that he was someone great, to whom they all gave heed, from the least to the greatest, saying, 'This man is the great power of God.' And they heeded him because he had astonished them with his sorceries for a long time."
(Acts 8:9-11)

In Acts 8, Simon Peter the apostle encountered Simon Magus the sorcerer. But before Peter meets Simon, there is an ironic comparison between Philip the evangelist and Simon the sorcerer. The same words go back and forth.

For a long time, the people of Samaria had "heeded" or "paid attention" to Simon and his deceptive sorcery (v11); now they "heeded" or "paid attention" to Philip and his miraculous signs (v6). Simon had "amazed" and "astonished" people claiming to be a great "power" from

God (v10); now Philip had "amazed" Simon when he saw the miracles and true "power" of God at work in him. The difference is that Simon was proclaiming himself as "great" (v9) and Philip was proclaiming the greatness of Jesus and His kingdom (v5, v12).

The Bible says that Simon had "practiced sorcery" or "practiced witchcraft" in that city. He used his "sorcery" for such a long time that people actually believed that he was "the great power of God." Anyone who claims to be great is surely deceived, because the only one who is truly great is Jesus Christ. We should all flee from someone "who boasts that he was someone great" (v9).

Various commentators have questioned the sincerity of Simon's conversion, but the Bible states clearly that "Simon himself also believed and he was baptized" (v13). What especially grabbed Simon's attention was "the miracles and signs which were done" by Philip in the power of the Holy Spirit. No doubt, Simon had operated for so long in supernatural satanic power, that he was drawn to the true power of God in the Spirit. This hunger for power, pride and prestige led to his downfall.

Many Samaritans were "born of the Spirit," but now the apostles from Jerusalem came so they could receive the "power of the Spirit." They laid hands on these new believers and "they received the Holy Spirit" (v17). They had been Spirit-saved, but not Spirit-baptized. Now they were baptized with the Holy Spirit. While this text does not say specifically, these Samaritans must have spoken in tongues or prophesied. Even though we cannot visually see the Holy Spirit, we can see His actions by various supernatural manifestations.

When "Simon saw that through the laying on of the apostles' hands the Holy Spirit was given, Simon offered them money" (v18). He said, "Give me this power also, that anyone on whom I lay hands may receive the Holy Spirit" (v19). As one commentator says, "He was not interested in bringing the Holy Spirit to others so much as in the power and prestige it would bring to himself. To bring the Spirit to others a man must be not a man of wealth but one who himself possesses the Spirit."[9] We must always keep in mind that "the Spirit's power is not a business transaction."[10] Simon did not want to be used by God in ministry for the glory of God; he wanted power. This is always dangerous, especially for a new believer.

This attempt to buy the gift of God brought a sharp rebuke from the apostle Peter. Listen to these fearful words from Acts 8:20-23: "Your money perish with you, because you thought that the gift of God could be purchased with money! You have neither part nor portion in this matter, for your heart is not right in the sight of God. Repent therefore of this your wickedness, and pray to God if perhaps the thought of your heart may be forgiven you. For I see that you are poisoned by bitterness and bound by iniquity." These words indicate that something was really wrong with Simon's spirit. Simon saw the Spirit's power; but Peter saw Simon's poison. He was "poisoned" and still in bondage ("captive to sin," NIV). His many years as a practitioner of the occult still permeated his thinking. His mind had not had time to be renewed to the ways of God, and his old ways as a sorcerer quickly surfaced. The long-term effects of witchcraft are difficult to break in people. Nothing but the power of God can set men free.

I believe that Simon was genuinely saved, and that is why Philip the evangelist baptized him (v13). And Simon received his salvation in an atmosphere of powerful preaching, supernatural miracles, signs and wonders, and "great joy." Acts 8:6-8 says, "Multitudes heard and saw the miracles which Philip did, for unclean spirits, crying with a

---

[9] *The Acts of the Apostles,* William Barclay, Daily Study Bible Series, Revised Edition, Westminster Press, Philadelphia, page 67.
[10] *Ancient Christian Commentary on Scripture,* Acts, Volume V, Edited by Francis Martin, InterVarsity Press, Downers Grove, Illinois, page 95.

loud voice, came out of many who were possessed; and many who were paralyzed and lame were healed. And there was great joy in that city." Simon was caught up with this excitement and got baptized along with many other "men and women."

I highlight Simon's conversion, because even though he was saved in the most powerful setting imaginable; even though miracles and healings took place all around him; even though he heard convicting and convincing messages about Jesus and His kingdom; Simon still needed personal discipleship and instruction in the ways of the Lord. When someone gets saved and delivered from a background of witchcraft, drugs, violence, gangs, or prison, he needs one on one oversight and care. It is so easy to revert back to old ways. If this person does not submit himself to local church leadership for accountability, he probably will not last long following Jesus Christ. He desperately needs a mature believer who can talk to him boldly and straightforwardly about the truth of God. These people have lived in lies for so long that only the truth of God in Christ can set them free.

YouTube Video: **The Christian and Witchcraft 02**

3

The Wizard of Indiana

As a young boy, I grew up watching the UCLA Bruins basketball team win one NCAA championship after another under the leadership of Coach John Wooden. For that and other reasons, I attended UCLA from 1978 through 1983. Because the UCLA campus is located in Westwood, California, Coach Wooden was known as "The Wizard of Westwood." There's even a book about him by that title.

I want to tell you now about "The Wizard of Indiana." I had never met a wizard before, but I had my opportunity through a series of incredible events back in 1988, when I lived in the state of Ohio. Here is what happened.

A very attractive 21-year old Christian lady was attending Indiana State University in Terre Haute, Indiana, about one-hour west of Indianapolis, the state capital. I could have never known that an encounter on this campus would lead to me meeting a wizard.

Linda[11] was walking down one of the pathways on campus. All of a sudden, a man in his mid-30s walked up to her. He definitely did not look like a student. He was wearing a long-sleeve shirt and a tie. He had a briefcase in his hand. He was clean shaven with short hair. He was also wearing a pair of thick glasses. Actually, he looked like one of the professors of the university.

"Hi. My name is Tom. You don't know me, but I know a little something about you."

This brief introduction immediately raised suspicions in Linda's mind because she had never seen this man in her life.

Over the next few minutes, he began telling her key details of events that had happened in her life. The man described people, places, and things from her past that no one else could have known except her. She was completely astonished. She thought to herself, "Could this man be a Christian? Does he have a true spiritual gift?"

Coming across as if he had a religious background, he said simply, "I have a gift given to me by God whereby I can tell people things about their past, present, and future. I've had this gift since I was a child."

This man continued talking to her in flattering language. In a calm way, he spoke about her good looks, intelligence, and potentially successful future. She was quickly drawn to his charm and nice words. Somehow, they arranged to meet again.

Over the next five or six weeks, they met several times on campus. He walked her to her classes. They had lunch together several times at the on-campus, fast food diners. She was completely swept off her feet by a man who was now telling her about her future. He was "predicting" incredible things to come.

---

[11] All the names in this story have been changed to protect confidentiality. The story is true.

As far-fetched as it sounds, she even began thinking about possibly marrying this man. She was a nominal Christian, but he seemed to have real favor with God, and it appeared that he had this mystical ability to know things about others. Again, were these gifts of the Spirit? Was he really a man of God?

She decided to invite him to meet her parents who lived in Dayton, Ohio, which was only a few hours east of the university. It was also where her good friend, Barbara, lived. Barbara was the Sunday School director of the church where I was the Associate Pastor.

A lot of red flags went off in Barbara's heart when Linda told her about Tom. She became even more alarmed after meeting him in person and hearing more of his story. Barbara found out that Tom had been married before – actually, several times. She found out that he had recently divorced his third wife, and he was only 35 years old.

When Barbara heard about Tom's "gifts," she probed a little deeper and found out that he was a wizard! He was a clairvoyant.[12] Barbara talked to Linda about immediately breaking off the relationship, and certainly not marriage. How could she be so blind to fall for a man who was not a servant of Christ, but a servant of Satan? Linda was so gullible, and she was falling in love with this man. He was so nice to her; why couldn't she maintain the relationship? She was confused.

There's another shocking piece to this story – before Barbara became a Christian, she was a practicing witch! She had been involved in witchcraft for many years, and she discerned all the evil behind Tom's life. She understood the world of wizards and witches.

---

[12] A clairvoyant is a psychic person who is supposedly able to perceive things about people and places beyond human reasoning and abilities. Tom was a servant of Satan.

Finally, a door of ministry opened up for Barbara. She found out that there was something that was really troubling Tom. It had to do with a recent dream that he had. Barbara asked him if he would be willing to come to her church and talk with her and one of the Pastors. My Pastor was out of town for the weekend, so I was the only one in the office. A meeting was arranged for Tom to see Barbara and me in the next few days.

Barbara called me with an excited voice. She told me the whole story, and said that a wizard wanted to come to our church and talk about a dream. We both agreed to pray and fast. I sensed that something big was getting ready to happen.

I wondered to myself – What does a wizard look like? Will he be dressed in a black cape with a pointy hat with astrological symbols? Will he have a wand in his hand? And then a really scary thought came to my mind: What if he zaps me with that wand and turns me into a frog?! Whoa! Do I want to do this? It sounds funny now, more than thirty-five years later, but back then, I was living with some genuine fear. I immediately started to fast and pray. God would see me through.

It was the middle of the week and I was the only one at the church. Barbara got there a few minutes before Tom and Linda pulled in to the parking lot. When I saw Tom wearing a tie with a sports coat and carrying a briefcase, I was completely surprised. This doesn't look like a wizard; he looked like your average insurance salesman. There was no wand or pointy hat! Good! I was safe.

After some brief introductions, we got right to the matter at hand.

"I have something that's been bothering me terribly for many months. I feel very frustrated and upset at myself. It has to do with a dream that I had a few months ago. I've had many special dreams in my life," Tom said. Then he added this specific part, "But I've always been able to interpret the meaning of my dreams. This recent dream is troubling me, because I know it has an important message for me, but I can't, for the life of me, interpret what it means."

Barbara said to Tom, "Tell us the dream."

"Well, in this dream, there was a one-bedroom house. I could see the inside of it. The walls of the room were painted white, but I noticed that the window shudders were closed, and you could not look out and no one could look in. Also, and this is very important, I saw two women dressed in white sitting in rocking chairs. Both of them were rocking back and forth."

Tom continued, "Then, all of a sudden, the one door to the room burst open. A bright light came flashing through. Abruptly, without warning, Evangelist Billy Graham appeared at the door announcing some type of good news. I couldn't make out everything he was saying, but I just understood that he was speaking something good into that room where the two women were sitting. With that, the dream ended."

"I have been pounding my brain over and over again trying to figure out what it all means. It has to be something important because I remember all the details."

Without hesitation, Barbara said, "I know what the dream means."

"You do?" asked Tom.

"Yes, while you were telling us the dream, the Lord was giving me the interpretation to it. All of the symbols in that dream are very specific to your life."

I noticed that Tom's eyes widened, and he couldn't wait to hear what Barbara would say.

"First of all, those two women represent your mother and grandmother. They are witches, aren't they?"

Tom was shocked. He said, "Yes, they are? How did you know?"

Barbara then said, "The reason the window shutters were closed was because everything these two women do is in secret. They are trying to hide their witchcraft from others. But God sees everything."

She added, "The reason the walls are all white is because these women think that what they are doing is all good. They think it's clean. And the reason Billy Graham showed up was to announce to these two ladies and to you, that the true light and salvation are in Jesus Christ. God is calling you out of this darkness, and telling you to come to the light that was surrounding Billy Graham. He wants you to repent and be saved. Give up your witchcraft and turn to the living God."

When Barbara finished, you could feel the power of God in the church office. Everything that Barbara said was true and Tom knew it. He stood there (he never sat down) with his mouth open. It was a moment of stunned silence. I sensed that he became aware that the dark power that was at work in him was no match for the power of God at work in Barbara. There was a feeling of complete resignation in Tom. It's over. You have been totally exposed and there's nowhere to hide.

He asked, "Why could you interpret it and not me?"

Barbara said, "Because God was waiting for this moment. The interpretation of this dream has been kept from you. The Lord wanted you to meet some Christians who could tell you about Christ and His salvation. This is all the plan of God. I don't have anything within myself to know how to interpret dreams. In the Bible, God gave people like Joseph and Daniel the ability to interpret dreams. What happened just now was a demonstration to all of us that God knows everything about you, and He wants you to come to Him."

To make a long story short, I led Tom in a prayer of salvation. I also told him to renounce his life as a wizard, and reject the ugly legacy of witchcraft left by his mother and grandmother. After Tom prayed, we all noticed an immediate change in his countenance. He was visibly shaken by God's power, and his face lit up the room. He was changed!

<u>*YouTube Video*</u>: **The Christian and Witchcraft 03**

THE CHRISTIAN & WITCHCRAFT

4

Elymas the Sorcerer

Acts 13:4-12

*"Elymas the sorcerer (for so his name is
translated) withstood them, seeking to turn the
proconsul away from the faith."*
(Acts 13:8)

Throughout the Book of Acts, is it not significant that the first opposition God's ministers encountered were always people involved with witchcraft? The first person to leave Jerusalem to spread the gospel was Philip, and he faced Simon the sorcerer. In the first missionary journey in Acts, the first enemy Paul and Barnabas confronted was Elymas the sorcerer. Right after the Macedonian vision and call to go to unknown regions, Paul and Silas met a woman with a fortune-telling spirit. Witchcraft is an enemy of the gospel message. It opposes the forward move of God into new areas.

Anointed "prophets and teachers" were gathered at "Antioch" to "fast and pray" and seek the direction of the Lord. The "Holy Spirit" called out "Saul (Paul) and

23

Barnabas" for a special "work" that He wanted done. The other ministers "laid hands" on these two and they were "sent out by the Holy Spirit."[13]

Saul and Barnabas boarded a ship that was sailing to the nearby island of "Cyprus." The first city they arrived at was "Salamis." The people there were very receptive to the gospel message. As they traveled east to west through the "island," they reached the city of "Paphos." The first person they meet was "a certain sorcerer, a false prophet, a Jew whose name was Bar-Jesus."[14] The Greek word here for "sorcerer" (also in verse 8) is "magos." It is the word for "magician." The only other place it appears in the NT is in Matthew Chapter 2 when it speaks of the "wise men"[15] who looked for the young child, Jesus.

You are told three other things about him: He was a Jew, a false prophet, and his name was "Bar-Jesus," or "son of Jesus." Is it not amazing that God's law can command His people to put to death any Jew if they practice witchcraft,[16] and here we have "a Jew" living as a sorcerer? Very often the Jewish people strayed far from God's commandments! Also, it's safe to say that every "sorcerer" is "a false prophet." No matter how convincing their predictions are, they are always false because it is not coming from the Holy Spirit but an evil spirit. They are using a false demonic power, not the true power of God. And finally, this "Jesus," the father of this sorcerer, was obviously not the Lord Jesus Christ. There were many Jewish people throughout the Mediterranean world that were named "Jesus" (Greek) or "Joshua" (Hebrew). So "Elymas" (v8) had a father named "Jesus." Occult practitioners always seem to have some "appearance of godliness,"[17] to quote

---

[13] See Acts 13:1-4.
[14] See Acts 13:6.
[15] See Matthew 2:1, 2:7 and 2:16 (2X).
[16] See Exodus 22:18.
[17] See 2 Timothy 3:5.

Paul's words. Nearly everyone involved with witchcraft that I've met has told me that they believe their gifts and abilities were from "God."

The well-known "gifted spiritual healer,"[18] Pat Longo, who trained and released the "Long Island Medium," Theresa Caputo, has the words "…and God gave some the gift of healing" on her website. This is a quote from 1 Corinthians 12:28. Here is a bona fide practitioner of Satan proclaiming herself as a woman sent by God! This is absurd. She, along with many others, has been sent to deceive.

We're not told why, but "Elymas" worked for the governor or proconsul of the island, "Sergius Paulus." Acts 13:7 specifically tells us that he was an "intelligent" man. He was very smart. He invited "Saul and Barnabas" to come to him so he could "hear the word of God" from them. The Lord had put a hunger[19] in Sergius Paulus for the things of God.

A very violent opposition surfaced. Acts 13:8 says, "Elymas the sorcerer *withstood* them, seeking to turn the proconsul away from the faith." "Elymas," a word of either Arabic or Aramaic origin, literally means "wizard." So, "Elymas the sorcerer" is "the wizard, the magician" (magos). He "withstood" them is a very strong word in Greek. It's interesting to me that when Paul wrote in 2 Timothy 3:8, "Now as Jannes and Jambres *resisted* Moses, so do these also *resist* the truth: men of corrupt minds, disapproved concerning the faith," the two words translated "resist" is the same word used here for "withstood." The Egyptian sorcerers resisted Moses, and now Elymas is resisting Paul and Barnabas. Also, Paul would write that "Alexander the

---

[18] These are her words not mine. This is the opening advertisement on her website next to a picture of her.

[19] The Greek word here for "desired" or "sought" is "epezētēsen," which means "to crave," even to the point of demanding something. He was very hungry for a message from God.

coppersmith" had done him "much harm" and other Christians must "beware of him" because he "greatly *resisted* my words."[20] "Resisted" is the same Greek word as "withstood." The same word is again used in Galatians 2:11, as Paul "*withstood* Peter to his face" when the truth of the gospel was at stake. The point is that Elymas very angrily and strongly opposed God's messengers and sought to prevent Sergius Paulus from receiving the eternal salvation found in Jesus Christ. This is a very wicked thing.

It's as if the hair on Paul's neck stood up. Acts 13:9 says, "He looked the sorcerer right in the eye" or "glared angrily at the sorcerer."[21]

What Paul said next is one of the strongest reactions against a person in the entire Bible. Not only did he rebuke Elymas with words, he also cursed him with blindness in God's full authority! Verses 10-11 read, "'You are a child of the devil and an enemy of everything that is right! You are full of all kinds of deceit and trickery. Will you never stop perverting the right ways of the Lord? Now the hand of the Lord is against you. You are going to be blind, and for a time you will be unable to see the light of the sun.' Immediately mist and darkness came over him, and he groped about, seeking someone to lead him by the hand." Wow, what authoritative and weighty words and action!

Let these words embolden the servants of the Lord. God hates witchcraft and He also hates when someone tries to turn people away from Him. Paul would tell one church that when people "forbid us to speak to the Gentiles that they might be saved," "may God's wrath come upon them!"[22] The truth is Christians have God's backing to "withstand" the servants of Satan who are opposing God's work. The apostle John said that Jesus came to this earth "to destroy the

---

[20] See 2 Timothy 4:14-15.
[21] See the NLT and TLB.
[22] See 1 Thessalonians 2:16.

works of the devil." He wrote these words while talking about people who were "children of the devil."[23]

For many years, my in-laws lived a few hundred feet from a house that was owned by a palm reader/psychic. There was a large billboard in her front yard advertising her "readings" and "predictions." Every time I drove or walked past this house, I pronounced God's curse over that wicked business. "In the name of Jesus Christ, I curse the finances of this palm reader. I pray that they will dry up from the roots. I pray that no one will ever go into this house again seeking guidance from the devil. I pray that this woman will get saved and give her life completely to the Lord. I command in Jesus' name that this business shut down forever!" Others joined me in prayer against this psychic. Within a few short years, that lady shut down her evil business and the windows and doors were all boarded up! I believe God answered our prayers. We are dealing with agents of the devil who are seeking to deceive and corrupt the people of our neighborhoods.

What Paul said to Elymas, he said while he was "filled with the Holy Spirit" (v9). He called him literally in Greek, "a *son* of the devil." Friends, not everyone is a child of God. Jesus said that the devil is a "father" and John said, "This is how we know who the children of God are and who the children of the devil are," and then he added that "Cain belonged" to the devil.[24] Jesus told a parable where He said, "The good seed stands for the sons of the kingdom. The weeds (tares) are the sons of the evil one." Elymas was not a child of God. He was a son of the devil. Elymas' earthly father was a man named "Jesus," but his spiritual father was the devil himself. God is Creator of all, but not the Father of all.

---

[23] See 1 John 3:8-10.
[24] See John 8:44 and 1 John 3:10-12.

When Sergius Paulus saw that Elymas left his presence completely blind, he was "astonished" and he "believed" on the Lord. Nothing was going to prevent the governor from receiving Christ. Once again, the power of God easily prevailed over the power of the devil. Remember: Aaron's snake swallowed up the snakes of the Egyptian sorcerers.[25]

YouTube Video: **The Christian and Witchcraft 04**

---

[25] See Exodus 7:12.

5

Women and the Psychic Connection

D id you know that all palm readers are women? Did you know that all the nationally syndicated astrologers are women? Did you know that all the "Psychic Hotlines" and "Psychic Networks" are run by women? "Miss Cleo," one of the most popular psychics, is a black woman. The Long Island Medium is Theresa Caputo, a woman. One of the most famous psychics and astrologers of the 20th Century was Jeane Dixon. Joyce Jillson,[26] before she died in 2004 from kidney failure at the age of 58, was the official astrologer of Twentieth Century Fox Studios and the Los Angeles Dodgers baseball team. Nearly all the top executives for national pornographic magazines and websites are women.

---

[26] Jillson would advise movie executives when would be the best time astrologically to release films, including the first *Star Wars* on May 25, 1977.

After President Ronald Reagan was nearly assassinated in 1981 by John Hinckley, Nancy Reagan regularly consulted the astrologer, Joan Quigley, to get advice on how to protect her husband.

Former French President, François Mitterrand consulted astrologer Elizabeth Teissier about the Gulf War and other matters of state. Teissier, who has written several books on astrology, once created a show of daily horoscope readings for a French television channel and the *Astro Show* for viewers in Germany interested in astrology.

Go to your local bookstore or shop on-line, and you'll see all the women writing the books on psychic topics. Consider these best sellers – *Psychics, Healers & Mediums* by Jennifer Weigel, *The Psychic Pathway* and *Diary of a Psychic* by Sonia Choquette, *The Book of Psychic Symbols* by Melanie Barnum, *Psychic Development for Beginners* by Emily Stroia, and another book by that same title written by Natalie Nolan, *Gifted – A Guide to Mediums, Psychics, & Intuitives* by Lisa Anders, *Discover your Psychic Type* by Sherrie Dillard, *Are You Psychic?* by Debra Lynne Katz, *Led by Light: How to Develop your Intuitive Mediumship Abilities* by Rev. Joanna Bartlett, *Psychic Shield* by Caitlin Matthews, *Confessions of a Sunday School Psychic* by Linda Stirling, and one that is simply called *Psychic* by Jen Solis. Women, women, women.

In the Bible, we have the "prophetess Noadiah"[27] who opposed Nehemiah and his workers when they were rebuilding the walls of Jerusalem. There's a "Jezebel" in the NT and there's a "Jezebel" in the OT. Jesus said to one church, "You allow that woman, Jezebel, who calls herself a prophetess to teach and seduce My servants to commit sexual immorality."[28] And you have the original one in the OT, of whom King Jehu said to Joram, "How can there be

---

[27] See Nehemiah 6:14.
[28] See Revelation 2:20.

peace as long as all the idolatry and witchcraft of your mother Jezebel abound?"[29]

There are certain objects that psychics and occult practitioners of the New Age spiritual movement are using to proclaim "healing powers." Supposedly an ancient practice, some women are strategically placing "stones" and "crystals" on the bodies of people to construct an "energy grid" and thus release "healing energy." Hundreds of "metaphysical crystal shops" and websites are popping up everywhere in our country and on-line touting the supernatural abilities of "energy gemstones," "healing crystals," and even "crystal divination cards." All of these objects are clearly cursed objects of witchcraft.

I'll never forget one Sunday morning years ago when I was teaching a message on the gifts of the Spirit based on 1 Corinthians 12:1-11, that a lady walked into our service whom I had never seen before. She did not have a Bible, but the whole time I was talking about God's spiritual gifts, she sat there with a big smile on her face and looked as if she hung on every word I was speaking.

As soon as the service was over, she came straight to the front to talk to me.

"That was a very interesting message," she said. "You were definitely led by a spirit."

The words, "a spirit," immediately caught my attention. I'm not sure why, but I had a sense right away that she was not a Christian.

She continued, "Is there a way I can meet with you this week and show you some books that I found in the library? They are books that allow me to connect with the spirit world." With that comment, I knew I was dealing with someone who was dabbling in the world of the occult.

"Are you sure these are not books on the occult?" I asked. She shared some other things about crystals and

---

[29] See 2 Kings 9:22.

seeing shapes and contorted figures in mirrors. This definitely concerned me.

"No, no, no, they are very helpful to me," she reassured me. "This is all good, I promise."

Honestly, I didn't want to meet with this lady. She was probably in her late 40's or early 50's. I was now wondering in my mind how to get away from her.

I'm not sure why, but I told her to come the next day so I could talk to her. I thought, just maybe, the Spirit of God could deliver her from whatever occult involvement she was in.

On Monday, first of all, I determined that I was not going to let her into the church building. I never meet with a woman alone for any counseling anyway, but I thought I could quickly challenge this lady, and help her to get rid of her occult paraphernalia.

I set up a table with two chairs out in the grassy area of our church near the parking lot, and in plain view of all the cars passing on Fowler Avenue. She said she was bringing several books, so the table would be useful.

She arrived on time at 10:00 a.m., and I saw her pulling out many large books from her truck. They were books on astrology and crystals.

"I used to live in Arizona. My husband and I were together for many years. But once a friend of mine gave me some crystals, a lot of supernatural things started happening in my house. I began to see shadows in my house and human forms in the mirrors of our walls. My husband couldn't handle any of it, and he left me. We divorced recently." I was reminded again that witchcraft is marriage breaker number #1.

She continued telling me about some crystals that she poured a liquid on and they reacted, setting off various gases and smoke. She then told me about "seeing" certain objects on television screens, and these objects were trying to make contact with antennas here on earth so that they could contact beings in space.

That was enough for me.

"Ma'am, I'm sorry. I need to stop you. All of these books and crystal objects that you're working with are pure, unadulterated witchcraft. There is no doubt about it in my mind, you have been deceived by the devil into this occult participation. You need to throw this stuff into that big trash bin over there in the parking lot, and renounce your involvement with these crystals and these books."

"But Pastor, I feel like I've tapped into something powerful. God uses these things, doesn't He? I mean, I have seen and heard many powerful things happening around me as I've engaged these items," she said.

"No, this is deception. This is witchcraft. Where is Jesus Christ in all of this? Where is this in the Bible? The devil has destroyed your marriage, and he has you running around obsessed with the dark things of the New Age movement. I advise that you burn all of this occult material."

No amount of prodding or convincing moved her. She took up all of her stuff and loaded them again in her truck. I folded up my table and brought it and the chairs back into the church building. I went into the sanctuary and prayed for her. I prayed for protection over our church and me. Jesus prayed, "Deliver us from the evil one" and "My prayer is not that you take them out of this world but that you protect them from the evil one." I never saw her again.

I was disappointed that she did not turn away from her practices. I prayed that at least a seed was sown in her life. Perhaps somewhere down the road, she will repent and give her life to Jesus. Witchcraft is a demonic stronghold that is often difficult to break off of someone's life.

YouTube Video: **The Christian and Witchcraft 05**

6

A Fortune-Telling Slave Girl
Acts 16:16-24

*"Now it happened, as we went to prayer, that a
certain slave girl possessed with a spirit of
divination met us, who brought her masters
much profit by fortune-telling."*
(Acts 16:16)

In Acts 16:16, Paul and Silas encountered "a
certain slave girl possessed by a spirit of
divination." Literally in the Greek text this last
phrase is "a spirit of a python." In Greek mythology,
"Puthōn" was a huge serpent killed by Apollo at Delphi.
Today, we know pythons as nonvenomous snakes that are
constrictors. They kill their prey through suffocation.

This evil spirit allowed this girl to make "her
masters" a lot of money "by fortune-telling." Whenever
Paul and others "went to prayer" (v16), she followed them
making a true declaration: "These men are the servants of
the Most High God, who proclaim to us the way of
salvation" (v17). I wish practitioners of the occult would say
that about us today!

She did this for "many days," and Paul finally had enough. He was "greatly annoyed" or "greatly troubled," and he turned toward that slave girl and spoke "to the spirit" that was in her – "I command you in the name of Jesus Christ to come out of her" (v18). That powerful word of command set her free in that very moment – "And he came out that very hour" (v18).

Let it be clearly known right here that all the people who are involved in fortune-telling and palm reading are under the influence of an evil spirit. In fact, even "her masters saw that their hope of making a great deal of money was gone" when that spirit came out of her. When the evil spirit left, the money left too![30] When people visit psychics and palm readers, they are really being consulted by evil spirits. This is not just a natural phenomenon whereby a woman has some special intuition to predict the future; no, she is under the influence and direction of a demon.

And let it be known again that the power of God is always greater than the power of Satan. We are to cast out evil spirits from people who are involved in witchcraft. It's interesting to me that this young girl did not even ask to be delivered! Paul did it anyway. He cast out the spirit of python by the Spirit of God.

The devil and "her masters" did not like what happened. The angry reaction of these men caused Paul and Silas to be severely persecuted before "the magistrates" in the city of Philippi. They were stripped of their clothes, "beaten with rods," and "thrown into prison." The text at verse 23 says that "they had many stripes laid on them." They took a severe beating. To top it off, their feet were fastened "in the stocks." They were later delivered

---

[30] As David Williams writes, "With a nice touch of humor, Luke uses the same verb 'to go out' of both the spirit and the assets" (*Acts*, NIBC, page 286).

supernaturally by God through a "great earthquake" that "loosed everyone's chains" (v26).

What was meant for evil, God turned it around for good. The Philippian jailer and his entire family received Jesus Christ as Lord and Savior and were water baptized (even in the middle of the night) (verses 30-33). When Paul and Silas were sent to jail, that's exactly where the Lord wanted them. People got saved, and others heard them singing hymns of praise to God and they all experienced a supernatural "chain-breaking" deliverance. God is good, and no amount of witchcraft is going to stop God's people.

Make no mistake about it, when you start coming against demonic powers, you are going to experience spiritual attacks, fierce opposition, and open persecution. The devil wants people to stay bound to their evil ways and lies. God wants them free. You don't have to go look for people involved in witchcraft; they will come to you. Paul did not search out this slave girl; she came to him. Every instance of witchcraft that I've had to deal with has come to me. I never went looking for anything. God has protected me, and I've never had to give in to these evil spirits.

YouTube Video: **The Christian and Witchcraft 06**

7

Burning Sorcery Scrolls in Ephesus
Acts 19:17-20

*"Many of those who believed now came and
openly confessed their evil deeds. A number
who had practiced sorcery brought their scrolls
together and burned them publicly. When they
calculated the value of the scrolls, the total came
to fifty thousand drachmas."*
(Acts 19:18-19)

The biblical city of Ephesus was a center of witchcraft and demonic activity. In Acts 19, we see that there was a "temple" dedicated to the "great goddess Artemis." People yelled, "Great is Artemis of the Ephesians" (v27). It was from Ephesus that "all of Asia and the whole world worshipped" this false goddess. It was in Ephesus that "Demetrius the silversmith made silver shrines (idols) of Artemis" (v24). It was here that God did "unusual miracles by the hands of Paul" that "evil spirits went out" (v12) of many Ephesians. There were

39

also "Jewish exorcists" there who tried to cast out "evil spirits" from people in the name of Jesus and Paul (v13), but one "evil spirit" overpowered these false exorcists when the spirit "leaped on them," "overpowered them," and caused them to leave "naked and wounded" (v16). A false goddess, an idol maker, exorcists, and evil spirits – Ephesus was a wicked place.

It was to these Ephesians that Paul would write about "the prince of the power of the air, the spirit who works in the sons of disobedience," "the principalities and powers in heavenly places," "don't give place to the devil," "the works of darkness," "the wiles of the devil," "the fiery darts of the wicked one," and that we are "not wrestling against flesh and blood, but against principalities, against powers, against the rulers of the darkness of this age, against spiritual hosts of wickedness in the heavenly places." You truly need the "full armor of God" so you can "stand, and having done all, to stand."[31]

Many years later, Jesus had to warn this Ephesian church of "false apostles who are liars," "the deeds of the Nicolaitans," and that they had "left their first love."[32] These Christians were easily swayed by many false things.

Remember the revival that broke out in Ephesus in Acts 19:17-19? The believers there came to the apostles confessing "their evil deeds" and they "burned the scrolls of sorcery (magic)." When they "calculated" how much these scrolls were worth, they arrived at a total of "50,000 drachmas." One drachma was about a day's wages for a laborer. People spend a lot of money to get into bondage and confusion. Despite the great expense of these scrolls, they burned them. They didn't sell them. They didn't give them away. They burned all of them. Why pass on the curse to someone else?

---

[31] See Ephesians 2:2, 3:10, 4:27, 5:11, 6:11-12, and 6:16.
[32] See Revelation 2:1-7.

I can't emphasize enough – if you have any objects of witchcraft in your house, you need to burn them. They are cursed. They will bring evil things into your life.

I recall the man who had lived a very troubled life, but one day came to our church and was radically saved by Jesus. It had been some time since I had seen someone who was so dramatically transformed by Jesus Christ. The oppression and darkness left him that day. We learned that he was a very gifted musician. He had a lot of very expensive musical equipment in his house and in storage.

When he was lost in the world, he bought and listened to a lot of worldly music. He told me that he had rare record albums of many rock and roll groups from the 50's, 60's, and 70's. When I saw his music collection, I was convinced that he could get many thousands of dollars for them. However, those albums were from some of the most demonic groups you could imagine. Some of the recording artists had sold their souls to the devil. Others were heavily involved in mystical beliefs of various occult groups (including the Beatles).

After looking over his impressive collection, I said, "I think you should burn all of these records." The man stared at me in stunned disbelief.

"You're not serious, are you?" he asked.

"Yes, the best thing to do with these records is burn them or throw them in the trash."

Again, he stood there without saying a word. He asked, "But can't I sell these valuable collections to a dealer and make a lot of money?"

"Yes, you could," I responded, "but why pass on the curse to someone else?" I added, "In God's eyes, your stuff is worthless and all it has done is bring you into bondage." As Jesus told some men, "What is highly esteemed among men is an abomination in the sight of God."

That man could not bring himself to depart from his dark music. I'm sad to say, but he never continued on with the Lord. He went back to his old ways. The curse was in his house and his music kept him bound.

Internationally-known Bible Teacher, Derek Prince (1915-2003) tells the interesting story of how he had to remove a cursed object from his house.

Prince's British parents served overseas in India and China with the British Foreign Service. In fact, Prince was born in Bangalore, India. When the parents were stationed in China, they had to flee the country because of the famous "Boxer Rebellion" in 1900, which expelled Christian missionaries and Western people that the "Boxers" thought were trying to culturally take over China.

In the 1970s, at the height of his ministry's outreach and effectiveness, Prince noticed that he was starting to have serious financial problems in the ministry. Also, there was lot of strife and division between his ministry and others that were associated with him. In a moment of despair, he sought the Lord for answers through prayer and fasting.

While he was praying about these problems in the family room of his house, he looked at a wall that had various paintings and decorations. This wall had some very exquisite and ornate dragons that had been given to his parents as a gift for their years of service in China. His parents had handed them down to him as an heirloom. As he stared at the dragons, he heard a voice in his heart ask, "Who is the dragon in the Book of Revelation?" He immediately knew the answer. Satan is pictured as a "great, fiery red dragon" in Revelation, Chapters 12 and 13. Somehow, he knew in that moment of discernment and revelation, that these dragons had brought a curse upon his ministry.

He could have sold those dragons for a lot of money because they were made of expensive materials and had great historical value. But dragons are satanic symbols. Also, "snakes" (the devil came as a serpent in the Garden of Eden), "goats" (are the cursed people at Christ's left hand),

and "frogs" (were used in the plagues of Egypt) have been used by Satanists and occult practitioners over the centuries as symbols of witchcraft (see the detailed teaching on objects, artifacts, and symbols of witchcraft in the last chapter of this book). Despite the sentimental value these dragon artifacts had to Derek because of his parents, he knew he had to get rid of them.

When he threw these items away, there was an immediate positive change in the finances and relationships of his ministry. A curse had been lifted from him and his ministry.

YouTube Video: **The Christian and Witchcraft 07**

8

A Final Word

*"For your merchants were the great men of the
earth, for by your sorcery, all the nations were
deceived."
(Revelation 18:23)*

This first section was about witchcraft in the
New Testament. Most of the instruction was
from the Book of Acts. As I close, I want to
look at a few other verses in the New Testament that deal
with witchcraft.

Paul wrote in Galatians 5:19-21 that "the works of
the flesh are very evident," and then he lists many evil things
including "adultery," "idolatry," "murders," "hatred,"
"jealousies," and "heresies." In verse 20, he lists "sorcery."
Some translations have "witchcraft." Witchcraft is a work
of the flesh. The Greek word used here for "sorcery" is
"pharmakeia." It is where we get our English word for
"pharmacy." Pharmakeia literally means "use of drugs."
When people used "magic spells" or "drug potions" in those
days, it was "pharmakeia." With the massive drug world that
we have today, I wouldn't be hesitant to say that drug

addiction and drug dealing are forms of witchcraft. Physically and mentally, people using methamphetamines and opioids are under the control of a chemical that makes them high. Several people who have been addicted to these powerful drugs have told me that many times they felt "possessed."

The Book of Revelation says many things about "sorcery" and "sorcerers." After the devastating trumpet judgments in Revelation, Chapters 8 and 9, you would think that everyone would bow the knee, repent, and give God all the glory. Not so. Revelation 9:21 says there will be people who "did not repent of their murders or their *sorceries* or their sexual immorality or their thefts." Again, some translations use the word, "witchcraft," and the Greek word is "pharmakeia." In these last days, people are not going to repent of their sorceries.

Revelation 18:23 makes a scary statement. When John writes about "the great city Babylon" that is violently thrown down by God's judgment, he reminds us that "by your sorcery (pharmakeia) all the nations were deceived." And it is in Babylon that you find "the blood of prophets and saints, and of all who were slain on the earth" (v24).

Finally, the sorcerers will meet their terrible end. Revelation 21:8 and 22:15 lets us know that the "pharmakoi," the "sorcerers," will "have their part in the lake that burns with fire and brimstone." Sorcerers go to hell. "Those who are dogs and *sorcerers* and sexually immoral and murderers and idolaters, and whoever loves and practices a lie" are lost forever in the lake of fire. Palm readers, psychics, astrologers, wizards, and other occult practitioners may enjoy their magic arts now, but they will pay the ultimate price later.

Perhaps you at one time were involved in witchcraft. Maybe you've used tarot cards, Ouija boards, or played dungeons and dragons. Maybe you visited a palm reader or read horoscopes daily. It is possible that you used a lot of drugs (pharmakeia) over the years. Perhaps you presently own movies or books that have a lot of witchcraft (like the Harry Potter series). Maybe you have dream catchers in the bedrooms of your house. Maybe you still have rosary beads, religious candles or incense, or small statues of the Virgin Mary. It's remarkable how much witchcraft is all around us.

This is your time to renounce these things. It is time to burn these objects. This is time to remove these curses and snares from your life. Witchcraft is evil and you must deal ruthlessly with it. You cannot be passive. Act now, and rid your house and your life of these cursed objects.

Let me lead you in a prayer of renunciation and re-commitment to the Lord Jesus Christ.

"Father, I come to you right now in the name of Jesus Christ the Lord. I openly reject and renounce any and all of my involvement with witchcraft from my past or my present. Deliver me from evil and deliver me from every negative influence coming from witchcraft. I will actively and openly oppose it wherever I see it. I will not allow any items of witchcraft to come into my life or my home – no movie, no book, no cult, no object, no snake, no dragon, and no devil! I receive the Holy Spirit to make me pure and holy in God's eyes. I ask You, Lord, to forgive me and cleanse me from every sin of witchcraft. I fully embrace the truth, the way, and the life of Jesus Christ. I want nothing to do with the devil and his ways; I chose to deny myself, take up my cross daily, and follow Jesus. I ask for Your help and Your strength to overcome the temptations and sins of the evil one. In Jesus' name, amen!"

YouTube Video: **The Christian and Witchcraft 08**

Witchcraft in the Old Testament

In the first section, we looked at the four times in the Book of Acts that the apostles had to confront sorcerers or people involved with witchcraft. Peter had to rebuke Simon the sorcerer in Acts 8; Paul cursed Elymas the sorcerer for trying to turn the proconsul away from the Lord in Acts 13; Paul cast out "a spirt of python" from a slave girl in Acts 16; after a revival came to the city of Ephesus, many new believers had to burn their scrolls of sorcery in Acts 19. These biblical stories were interspersed with personal stories of confronting witchcraft from my ministry as a pastor. We concluded by looking in the Book of Revelation at the sorcerers and their sorceries.

In this second section, we will spend our time in the Old Testament (OT) and see what it says about sorcery. I want to emphasize the subject of "cursed objects." Many of the personal testimonies in this study will deal specifically with these objects.

Recall that we said at the beginning that the Old Testament (OT) uses sixteen different Hebrew words for "wizards," "mediums," "spiritists," "psychics," "necromancers," "sorcerers," "enchanters," "witches," "soothsayers," "diviners," "magicians," "astrologers," "observer of times," and those with "familiar spirits." The

49

New Testament (NT) has nine similar words. The Bible says a lot about these servants of Satan.

Let's start with a very vivid example that I experienced many years ago.

9

The Porcelain Buddha

I'll never forget what happened many years ago when I worked for a local medical company.

I supervised a small staff of five administrative workers. One of the ladies, a very hard worker, began to tell us of health problems with her son. He was seventeen years old and in excellent physical condition. He was one of the top swimmers at his high school. Suddenly, he got very sick. He would have fevers, colds, and chills off and on for months, even during the summer. He felt weakness throughout his body. They went to several different doctors, took many tests, but no one knew the cause and his condition remained. This lady and her husband were very concerned that perhaps some unknown illness would eventually kill their son.

Although she was not a Christian believer, she did talk about "God," and she knew that I was a Bible teacher at a local church. As she told me about her son's plight, I told her that I would definitely pray for him until his condition improved. Our church also began to pray.

I'll never forget what happened next. My regular weekly fasts were on Wednesdays, so I left work during the lunch hour and drove about ten minutes to my house so I could pray alone. As I was walking around praying in my kitchen and family room, suddenly, I saw in my mind's eye a picture of a porcelain Buddha figurine. I remembered that this lady had one in her cubicle at work. As soon as I "saw" that picture, I knew that was the answer. I read again that well-known portion of Scripture in Deuteronomy 7:26 about not bringing "cursed objects" into your house or you will become cursed like them.

We had employee policies in place at work that prohibited me as a supervisor from using my position to promote my Christian beliefs with subordinates. I realized I was taking a risk, but this lady knew me well enough to know that I wasn't an overbearing person with her when it came to these matters. I just needed to be obedient to what the Lord let me see.

Right after I got back to work, I asked her to come into my office. I closed the door behind me. I think that scared her a little bit because she felt like she was in trouble. I told her not to worry. I explained to her what had just transpired at my house. The more I talked, the more her eyes opened wide. Even her mouth opened wide. I then pulled out my Bible that was always on my desk and I read to her from Deuteronomy 7:26 while she looked on. "Nor shall you bring an abomination into your house, lest you be doomed to destruction like it. You shall utterly detest it and utterly abhor it, for it is an accursed thing." I told her that that Buddha statue in her cubicle had brought a curse into her family. If she would get rid of that little statue, her son would be healed. Even before I was done talking, she opened the door and immediately went to her cubicle and removed that Buddha.

She told me later that she took that porcelain figurine and smashed it in the large trash bin that was out in the parking lot. The Buddha shattering into a thousand pieces. *Within a few days, her son was totally healed!* This lady was so overwhelmed with joy that she immediately told me the news.

One thing I learned from this lady was that the porcelain Buddha was a gift to her from the personnel director of our company. Almost from the day she put that Buddha in her cubicle, her son got sick with fevers. She wasn't worshipping Buddha nor did she rub his belly hoping for good luck. It was simply a gift from a friend. She had no particular feelings either way about it.

I can tell you without a doubt that Deuteronomy 7:26 has been the one verse I have used over and over again when dealing with witchcraft in people's lives – believers and nonbelievers. Multitudes of people have brought untold curses into their lives because they have, often innocently, brought cursed objects into their houses. These have come by way of books, charms, amulets, jewelry, rings, fetishes, music, videos, movies, drugs, and many other things. I will say more about this later.

Recently, a man came to see me for counseling. God had been dealing with him about many things in his life. He had once served the Lord as a youth at his local church. Because of many unfortunate events in his life, he slowly turned away from the Lord.

In our discussions together at the church, he mentioned that he had a Buddha in his house. The Lord was already speaking to him about getting rid of it.

After we finished about ninety minutes of counseling, I went and got a written copy of the above testimony of the lady and her son who was sick because of the Buddha figurine in her cubicle.

He told me at our next meeting that after reading that story, he went home and got rid of the Buddha from his house.

He told me, "Pastor, guess what happened?"

"What?" I asked.

"After I got rid of that Buddha, my son came home and noticed something totally different about the atmosphere of our house."

Something was different, and the son noticed a "freedom" and "liberation" over the house.

"Guess what else happened?" he added.

"When my wife got home, she also mentioned that something felt totally different about the family room/house. When she looked over at where the Buddha once stood, she said to me, 'You got rid of it, didn't you?'"

"Pastor, something changed at my house. It feels different. It was like an oppression left us. It feels so much better at home."

Friends, get rid of any Buddhas or other cursed objects from your house. They bring in curses into your life.

YouTube Video: **The Christian and Witchcraft 09**

10

Cursed Objects
Deuteronomy 7:25-26

*"Nor shall you bring an abomination into your
house, lest you be doomed to destruction like it.
You shall utterly detest it and utterly abhor it,
for it is an accursed thing."
(Deuteronomy 7:26)*

The Book of Deuteronomy is all about God's commandments and obeying them. Deuteronomy 5 gives us the Ten Commandments and Deuteronomy 6 has the greatest commandment ("Love the Lord with all your heart, with all your soul, with all your strength"). Using a variety of verbs – "obey," "perform," "observe," "keep," "do," and "walk in" – the Lord and Moses commanded Israel in Deuteronomy to follow His "commandments" (132X), "statutes" (30X), "judgments" (20X), "ways" (12X), and "testimonies" (3X). "Obey," "obedience," "obedient," and "obeyed" are found in chapter after chapter. They were instructed repeatedly to "obey My commandments," "obey the commandments," "obey all these words," and the most frequent, "obey His voice" and "obey the voice of the Lord your God." "His voice" means that God is speaking, so His people must "hear," "listen," and "obey." God was speaking to all of Israel – "Hear, O Israel" (5:1), "Hear, O Israel" (6:3), "Hear, O Israel" (6:4), "Hear, O Israel" (9:1), and "Hear, O Israel" (20:3). The message is loud and clear: Pay attention; God is speaking to you!

The Lord was the "jealous God" (6:15) who demanded obedience to all of His law. They were to "fear Him," "serve Him," and "worship Him" alone. Jesus countered Satan's three temptations in the wilderness with "It is written" from three verses in Deuteronomy, concluding with "You shall worship the Lord your God, and Him *only* You shall serve."[33] The Lord tolerated no rivals. His people were to worship Him alone. No idols were allowed. The truth is that there are no other gods. All the other gods are false because they don't exist. The only God is the God of Israel. The first commandment was the most important – "You shall have no other gods before Me" (5:9). I'm number #1. There's not even a number #2. Your whole life must revolve around Me. I am your life, God was saying to them.

When you get to Deuteronomy, Chapter 7, the Lord was instructing them on what to do when they got into the Promised Land. The people of the land of Canaan were idolaters. Their land was full of idols. They participated daily in abominable practices. They "practiced witchcraft," "consulted sorcerers," "sought mediums," and "visited spiritists." It was a superstitious culture that thrived on idolatry, wickedness and sorcery.

So now we get to the verses in question, Deuteronomy 7:25-26. Breaking it down phrase by phrase, here is what you find:

- "You shall burn the carved images of their gods with fire." He had already written earlier, "burn their

---

[33] See Matthew 4:1-10, especially verse 10.

carved images with fire" (7:5) and will say it again later, "burn their wooden images with fire" (12:3). When you burn something, you plan to completely destroy it. It can't be used again. This is what God wants us to do with all items of witchcraft – burn them! We will say this again and again in these teachings on witchcraft. Burn everything; thus, no one will be able to get their hands on it and use it again.

- "You shall not covet the silver or gold that is on them." I have met many people who have valuable collections of books, artifacts, music, movies, and jewelry. To sell these items to collectors or others would generate a lot of money for them. But the Lord says, "Do not covet." Even though the "scrolls of sorcery" in Ephesus were worth 50,000 drachmas of silver in Acts 19 (worth millions of dollars today), the believers there "burn them" in the fire (19:19).

- "Nor take it for yourselves, lest you be snared by it." All snares are traps. They allure you through deception, but in the end, they put a hook in you and it is nearly impossible to escape. The cursed objects of witchcraft bind you directly to what is evil. Fishermen use hooks, fowlers use traps, and hunters use snares to capture their prey. The fish, birds, and animals are soon killed and devoured. Witchcraft does that to its victims.

- "For it is an abomination to the Lord your God." The word, "abomination," is the strongest word in the English language for hatred. To abominate something means that you really, really hate it intensely. God really hates idolatry, idols, and items of witchcraft. And notice that it is "an abomination *to the Lord your God.*" So often, other people, especially unbelievers, think everything is just fine. Jesus once said, "For what is highly esteemed among

57

men is an abomination in the sight of God."[34] There are many things and behaviors that men praise, but God hates.

- "Nor shall you bring an abomination into your house, lest you be doomed to destruction like it." So many people – often innocently – bring cursed items right into their house. Books, music, movies, religious candles, jewelry, tarot cards, games, crystals, amulets, and other paraphernalia are brought into homes without realizing that curses, darkness, and evil just came through the doors. *Don't bring anything into your house that God hates.* It is an abomination. God hates it. Don't make God angry. Here's why: It's for your own good. You will be "doomed to destruction" just "like it." Why bring a cursed object into your house and become cursed? A classic biblical example is Achan in Joshua 7, who brought the "accursed thing"[35] into his tent and caused all of Israel to be defeated by its enemies. One man's sin caused the entire army to be defeated. They became cursed like the objects Achan coveted. Joshua 22:20 reads, "Did not Achan the son of Zerah commit a trespass in the accursed thing, and wrath fell on all the congregation of Israel? He was not the only one who died for his sin." All of Israel suffered and Achan was not the only one who died. What should have been offered up to God in sacrifice, he kept for himself. (I will deal extensively with this subject in the last chapter of this book.)
- Finally, "You shall utterly detest it and utterly abhor it, for it is an accursed thing." God's hatred must

---

[34] See Luke 16:15.
[35] See Joshua 7:13, 7:15, and 22:20; 1 Chronicles 2:7. He took "a beautiful Babylonian garment, two hundred shekels of silver, and a wedge of gold weighing fifty shekels" (Joshua 7:21).

become ours. No stronger language can be found – "utterly detest" and "utterly abhor." *Whatever is an abomination to God must be an abomination to us.* The reason we are to hate it is because "it is an accursed thing." It's going to bring curses into your life. It's going to destroy you. It's going to bring all kinds of bad things into your family, finances, marriage, children, and spiritual life. You must hate what God hates.

Year after year, I find Christians with cursed objects in their homes. They are items of witchcraft. Many believers think that they are innocent items that will cause no harm. They are sadly mistaken. I owned many of these items before I knew Christ. I had to get rid of them as I came to understand their evil origins.

<u>YouTube Video</u>: **The Christian and Witchcraft 10**

THE CHRISTIAN & WITCHCRAFT

11

Dream Catchers and the Little Girl

I don't go looking for demons or witches, but they sure have come looking for me. While I have studied this subject extensively in the Bible and researched it through various books and articles, I would not consider myself an expert by any imagination. However, as a Christian and as a Pastor, I have confronted witchcraft in many situations. I'm amazed how subtle and sly this has become, and many gullible Christians are accepting it with no regard to the serious ramifications involved.

One day I received a call from a lady in our church. She wanted to know if I would go visit a relative that was having some strange things happening in her house.

"What's going on?" I asked.

She told me that this family would regularly hear cabinet doors open and close in the kitchen even though no one was in there. Also, and more concerning, one of the young daughters – a six-year-old – would tell her parents that she would speak to a dead relative, a grandmother, who would come and talk to her. The girl's mother would often stand by the door of her room and hear her little daughter talking to someone.

I definitely thought something demonic was happening in that house. I agreed to go over.

I found the family to be very friendly. As usual, when I suspect witchcraft, I look around the house at the walls, pictures, or bookcases for any objects that might bring a curse. I did notice right away some very bad video games that I knew were violent and evil. They had some games that glorified the killing of police officers, but this was not my biggest area of concern.

I asked a lot of questions. The mom answered every question as best she could. She began to tell me how her little girl had been talking to the "grandmother" for some time. She described all the interactions. Then I asked this key question that I always ask when I'm dealing with witchcraft: *Has there been any object brought into the house or her room when all of this started happening?* The only thing she could think of was a dream catcher that was placed on one of the walls next to her bed.

That was it, I thought. I then asked, "Can I go to her room?"

"Yes, of course," she said.

The room looked like a very typical bedroom of a young girl. It was clean and orderly. There was a bed on the right side. I noticed the dream catcher on the opposite wall. Nothing else looked out of place or remarkable. As I walked into her room, three things happened immediately: 1) I felt a heaviness in the room, almost like my breathing was labored, 2) I started to sweat profusely. This never happens to me unless it's the middle of summer and I'm in a very hot place, and 3) the hair on both of my forearms stood straight up (I even showed them to the other people who walked in with me). I felt an evil presence in that room. I told the mother to get rid of the dream catcher. I also spent time praying in the room and over the little girl. I instructed her not to speak to that "voice" that she was hearing but to reject it in the name of Jesus. After praying, I thanked the family for inviting me and I left. I heard recently that nothing more has happened with the little girl or the cabinet doors.

Dream catchers have come to us from the Native American Indians. There are several different legends regarding dream catchers. In the next four paragraphs, you'll find the version based on the Lakota legend:

"An old Lakota spiritual leader[36] was on a high mountain and had a vision. In his vision, Iktomi, the great trickster and searcher of wisdom, appeared in the form of a spider. Iktomi spoke to him in a sacred language. As he spoke, Iktomi the spider picked up the elder's willow hoop which had feathers, horsehair, beads and offerings on it, and began to spin a web. He spoke to the elder about the cycles of life.

As he continued to spin his web, Iktomi said that in each time of life there are many forces, some good and some bad. If you listen to the good forces, they will steer you in the right direction. But, if you listen to the bad forces, they'll steer you in the wrong direction and may hurt you. So, these forces can help or they can interfere with the harmony of nature. While the spider spoke, he continued to weave his web.

When Iktomi finished speaking, he gave the elder the web and said, 'The web is a perfect circle with a hole in the center. Use the web to help your people reach their goals, making good use of their ideas, dreams and visions. If you believe in the great spirit, the web will catch your good ideas and the bad ones will go through the hole.'

The elder passed on his vision to the people and now many Indian people have a dream catcher above their bed to sift their dreams and visions. The good is captured in the

---

[36] This is basically a witch doctor.

web of life and carried with the people, but the evil in their dreams drops through the hole in the web and are no longer a part of their lives. It is said that the dream catcher holds the destiny of the future."[37]

Let me summarize – dream catchers started when a witch doctor had a vision of a spider spinning a web that could be used to determine a person's future if he "believed in the great spirit." These catchers hold your future destiny in their hands, they say.

For true Christian believers, this is foolish. This is also demonic. It is a cursed object that deceptively works its way into homes to bring curses. Throw that dream catcher into the fire or nearest trash can.

YouTube Video: **The Christian and Witchcraft 11**

---

[37] These paragraphs are from the *dream-catchers.org* website.

12

Those Who Practice The Occult
Deuteronomy 18:9-19

*"There shall not be found among you anyone
who makes his son or his daughter pass through
the fire, or one who practices witchcraft, or a
soothsayer, or one who interprets omens, or a
sorcerer, or one who conjures spells, or a
medium, or a spiritist, or one who calls up the
dead."*
(Deuteronomy 18:10-11)

O nce again, here in Deuteronomy, Chapter 18, the Lord is concerned with how the inhabitants of Canaan will influence His people with their evil customs and practices. Don't "learn" or "imitate" what these people do. God is emphatic – "Don't follow the abominations of those nations" (v9). For "abominations," other translations use words like "hateful things," "horrible customs," "detestable ways," "terrible things," and just plain, "disgusting." The bottom-line: God says, *I hate what they do.*

In verses 10-11, we have a list of eight types of occult practitioners that the people of Israel were strictly forbidden to visit or become. Here's the list of people:

- "Who practices witchcraft" – This is a blanket statement forbidding any type of witchcraft. Different translations use words like "divination," "sorcery," "fortune-telling," and "black magic." The Hebrew word here for "witchcraft" is the same word used to describe the type of "divination" that Balaam practiced.[38] It's the same word used in the phrase, "Rebellion is as the sin of *witchcraft*" in 1 Samuel 15:23.

- "Soothsayer" – By definition, a soothsayer is someone who can supposedly tell or predict future events. The prophet Daniel was challenged by "soothsayers" in Babylon and Balaam was known as "the soothsayer."[39] Down at verse 14, it reads, "these nations listened to soothsayers."

- "One who interprets omens" – An omen is when something happens to someone that is seen as a sign of that person's future. Again, this has to do with predicting future events.

- "Sorcerer" – Exodus 22:18 reads, "You shall not permit a *witch* to live." The Hebrew word here for "witch" is the same as "sorcerer." Pharaoh called his "wise men and *sorcerers*" to turn their staffs into snakes in Exodus 7:11. The Lord said through the prophet Malachi that He would bring "quick judgment" against "sorcerers" because "they do not fear Me."[40]

- "Conjure spells" – This person tries to invoke evil, supernatural powers to influence or curse others

---

[38] See Numbers 22:7 and 23:23.
[39] See Daniel 2:27, 4:7, 5:7, and 5:11; Joshua 13:22.
[40] See Malachi 3:5.

through pronouncing of spells or curses. I remember going to the island nation of Haiti – where a lot of voodoo is practiced – and seeing how the witch doctors would put objects like rice in bowls together with chicken bones at intersections and invoke spells so that their enemies would have accidents at those very intersections.

- "Medium" and "one who calls up the dead" – A medium is someone "who stands in the middle" and believes she can transmit messages between a living person and the spirits of the dead. The witch at Endor – that King Saul consulted – was such a person. She was a medium and a necromancer. A "necromancer" is a person who tries to communicate with the spirits of the dead to influence the future. The KJV translates "necromancer" as "one who calls up the dead." When the witch called up the spirit of the departed Samuel, he predicted that the death of Saul and his sons would happen the next day.[41]
- "Spiritists" – This word is translated "psychics" by one translation and "wizards" by many others. It is a person who uses the power of Satan or witchcraft to advance evil purposes. 2 Kings 21:6 says that King Manasseh "made his son pass through the fire, practiced soothsaying, used witchcraft, and consulted *spiritists* and mediums. He did much evil in the sight of the Lord to provoke Him to anger." He was not the only king to do so.

That was an ugly list. Deuteronomy 18:12 says, "For all who do these things are an abomination to the Lord." Notice that it says "all who do" – not the act, but the actual person – are an abomination. And it's because of these "abominations" that God drove these people out from before

---

[41] See 1 Samuel 28:3-19.

THE CHRISTIAN & WITCHCRAFT

the Israelites.   Verse 13 calls on God's people to be
"blameless" and "innocent." "Never be guilty of doing any
of these disgusting things," one translation says.[42] It closes
in verse 14 by saying that "God has not appointed diviners
and soothsayers for you."

I believe that these people – soothsayers, wizards,
mediums, necromancers, spiritists, and sorcerers – do not
have any special abilities of their own. They are working
directly with demons. These are evil spirits sent from Satan
himself to bind, confuse, and deceive people. To consult any
of these evil people is to immediately come under Satan's
influence and bondage. He is a deceiver and a liar. He is the
father of lies.

I think it is tremendously significant that right here
in the middle of talking about all these practitioners of
witchcraft, Moses talks about Jesus Christ. In the very next
verses, Deuteronomy 18:15-19, Moses said that "God would
raise up a Prophet like me" and God would "put His words
in His mouth, and He shall speak everything I command,"
and if anyone does not "listen to that Prophet," God "will
personally deal with anyone who will not listen to the words
the Prophet proclaims on My behalf."[43] When the apostle
Peter was witnessing to some Jewish people about the Lord
Jesus Christ in Acts 3:22-23, he reminded them that "Moses
truly said to the fathers, 'The Lord your God will raise up for
you a Prophet like me from your brethren. Him you shall
hear in all things, whatever He says to you. And it shall be
that every soul who will not hear that Prophet shall be utterly
destroyed from among the people.'" Jesus is "that Prophet."

A Christian believer never has to consult anyone
involved in witchcraft. We have Jesus Christ. He knows the
future. We have the Holy Spirit and "He will tell us things
to come." We have the gifts of the Spirit that include

---

[42] See CEV translation.
[43] See Deuteronomy 18:15, 18-19.

"prophecy," "words of wisdom and words of knowledge," and "discerning of spirits." We have the Word of God, the Bible. Everything that Christians need can be found in God and His Word. We don't need any horoscopes, palm readers, tarot cards, wizards, or psychics to tell us about our past, present or future. We have the Lord, and He is more than enough!

<u>*YouTube Video*</u>: **The Christian and Witchcraft 12**

THE CHRISTIAN & WITCHCRAFT

13

Halloween Paraphernalia

I will never forget how tired and distressed this lady looked. She had four children.[44] They were in stair-step order – seven, five, three, and one. They were very cute kids, but they had big problems. *They were always sick. They always had accidents.* It seemed that this lady lived at the local emergency room of the nearest hospital. One kid would get pink eye, then another would come down with a cold. One would develop pneumonia, then another would cut his head against a table that would require stitches. One would have a terrible rash break out over his whole body, while another would break her wrist after taking a bad fall on the sidewalk. It was one calamity after another, and this mother was tired and weary of it.

"Pastor Charlie, I need help. I can't take it anymore."

I responded, "Tell me what's happening."

She said – and notice the wording – "I feel like we're living *under a curse*. My kids are always sick. They can't

---

[44] Her husband had spent time in prison. At the time this mother was attending our church, her husband was living with another woman.

stay well. It seems like our house is *plagued by bad luck.* We are *accident prone.*" I could hear the anguish and heartache in her voice.

"Can I come over and talk to you?"

"Yes, please come," she said. And again, she said, "I can't take it anymore."

I arranged a time to visit her apartment on a weekend when all the kids were home.

When I went into her apartment, I immediately started to look around to see if I could find anything obvious. I didn't see anything of concern. I began to ask her a lot of questions. Finally, after poking and prodding here and there, I hit a nerve. By chance, I touched on the subject of Halloween. When I mentioned Halloween, she got really excited and told me about all of the special costumes she had in her closet for all her kids. There it was!

The closet happened to be in the very family room where I was sitting. When she opened that closet it was like a witch's laboratory! She not only had very expensive and sophisticated masks of demons, skeletons, vampires, etc., but she also had books on candle lighting, witches' brews, crystals, and magic. This lady was very well versed in many areas of the occult. This had been a big part of her life before she become a believer and started attending our church.

I told her very plainly that these objects and books were the source of her problems. We needed to burn all of them right away! She didn't have much of a yard at this small apartment, so I had to figure out a way to get rid of all this paraphernalia without causing a large bonfire! Finally, I realized that her apartment was near a large shopping mall that had large trash dumpsters in the back. I decided to load all of those demonic costumes and books into the trunk and back seats of my car. It literally filled that trunk to capacity. I didn't want to drive too far because "the curse" was now in my car! Thank God, those trash bins were only a few hundred feet away. I went and dumped all of that stuff into the trash. I felt unclean just touching everything.

I can't say that everything changed for that lady on that day, but over the next few months, all of the troubles stopped that she and her kids had been experiencing. The curse was removed and the power of the enemy was broken.

Once again, Deuteronomy 7:26 was at work. If you bring cursed objects into your house, they will bring unseen curses into your life. When I use the word "unseen," I'm saying that many times it will not be obvious to you that the cursed object is causing most of the problems. You'll just think you're having a string of bad luck. You'll suddenly start having accidents. You'll burn your hand in the kitchen. Your tire will blow out on the truck. The washer stops working and you need it repaired. The kids start getting sick. They'll get well one week, and the next week, they're all sick again. You make regular visits to the doctor and emergency room. It's a never-ending cycle of bad breaks and frustrating setbacks.

As I mentioned earlier, I was a supervisor at a local medical company many years ago. One of ladies that I worked with was a data entry tech. This Christian lady sat daily in her cubicle and entered thousands of numbers, names, and personal information at a data terminal. She was very good and rarely made any errors.

One day, completely out of the blue, she walked into my office and sat down in the chair in front of my desk. Right away she asked, "Will you pray for me?"

"Yes, of course, is there anything specific? Are you okay? You look quite worried?"

"I don't understand it. I've had a reoccurring problem in my life for many years and I've never known how to resolve it," she said.

The way she was talking to me sounded like she was hesitant to disclose the problem. For some reason, I had this bad feeling that she was getting ready to tell me something very private and personal. Maybe she was having an affair, I thought. Maybe she was doing something illegal, and I would have to get my boss involved and possibly even the police. A lot of wild thoughts began to race through my mind.

Finally, she said, "I have terrible nightmares nearly every night. I don't know how to stop them. I mean, these are terrible nightmares and I often wake up drenched in sweat and even screaming. It scares my husband. I don't know what to do about it. Please pray for me."

"Yes, I will pray, and I'll ask my church to pray for you."

With that, she got up and walked back to her cubicle.

I don't know if it was within several days or even a few weeks, but I remember one day as I was praying for her, a strong impression entered my mind that she was putting bad images in her heart and mind on a regular basis.

Then I thought about ways in which people get digital or visual images into their head. What are people doing? I thought about men who view pornography on the Internet or through magazines, videos, and movies. Again, I had a strong inner impression that she was watching something on television or through movies.

The next time I saw her, I asked, "Barbara,[45] do you by any chance watch scary movies? Movies on vampires or movies like *Psycho, Night of the Living Dead, The Exorcist,* or movies that involve witchcraft. Have you seen *The Shining, Texas Chainsaw Massacre, Rosemary's Baby, Jaws, Halloween, Carrie,* and *Willard?*" These were many of the famous horror movies from the 1970s.

Barbara immediately got excited. "Yes, I love all those movies. Horror movies are my favorite type of movies. I like the suspense. I like to get scared."

---

[45] This is not her real name to protect confidentiality. The story is true.

I couldn't believe that she couldn't make the association between her movies and the nightmares.

"Don't you realize that you are putting all of those evil, horror images into your spirit. Those images are staying in your heart and mind. They are being imprinted into your brain. No wonder you have nightmares. No wonder you wake up with screams."

Barbara told me that she had a vast collection of these videos in her house – 100's of videos. It would be safe to say that she personally owned probably every horror flick that was available. She spoke of these movies as her "library."

She was more than a little bit shocked when I said, "You need to get rid of them. You need to burn them."

"You also need the Holy Spirit to cleanse, purge, and wash your heart and mind from all those evil images. Your thoughts and imaginations have been defiled with a lot of fear, violence, brutality, savagery, killings, stabbings, witchcraft, and other demonic stuff. It's like you have been contaminated, but with God, nothing is impossible."

Over the course of many months, she stopped watching the horror movies. Slowly but surely, she began to throw away her movies. It was very hard to do. This is what she watched for many years. *But the nightmares stopped.* As she prayed, her mind was cleansed.

While I'm on this subject of horror movies, I remember years ago mediating on Proverbs 6:18. This verse says that God hates "a heart that devises wicked imaginations or wicked schemes." There were seven things that were an abomination to the Lord, and this was one of them. I used to watch a lot of documentaries on true crimes – *FBI Files*, *Forensic Files*, and criminal investigations. These TV programs would reenact brutal murders, sadistic killings, and even violent rapes and stabbings. The people who do these terrible crimes "devise wicked imaginations" in their minds. What do you think a movie director or producer is doing with horror movies? His mind and heart are contriving terrible scenes of fear, violence, killings, and even satanic involvement. Why would I want to subject my spirit to these kinds of images? My body is the temple of the Holy Spirit. We must guard our heart and not allow anything in that defiles and corrupts our thinking.

YouTube Video: **The Christian and Witchcraft 13**

14

Witchcraft Defiles
Leviticus 19:31, 20:6-7, and 20:27

*"Give no regard to mediums and familiar
spirits; do not seek after them, to be defiled by
them: I am the Lord your God. And the person
who turns to mediums and familiar spirits, to
prostitute himself with them, I will set My face
against that person and cut him off from his
people."*
(Leviticus 19:31, 20:6)

The Book of Leviticus is often difficult for
Christians to read because it has so many gory
details about "burnt offerings," "grain
offerings," "peace offerings," "sin offerings," and "trespass
offerings." None of these "offerings" seem relevant to us
living in our day. This instruction was for priests living
under the Mosaic law of sacrifices and offerings to God.

However, Leviticus really shows us God's holiness
and His standards for living. Leviticus helps us discern the
true nature of sin and its consequences. This book gives us

THE CHRISTIAN & WITCHCRAFT

the famous saying, "You shall be holy, for I am holy."[46] If you want to understand what God believes about sexual immorality – sins like incest, rape, adultery, fornication, homosexuality, and bestiality – just read Leviticus. Paul was right: "By the law is the knowledge of sin."[47] If you are not sure whether some behavior is a sin, just look at this book.

Leviticus, Chapters 18 and 19, show you what is sinful in God's eyes; Leviticus, Chapter 20, shows you the punishment for such sins. In other words, if you do what is evil, here is the penalty for your wicked action. Many of the sins, especially sexual sins, were punishable by death.

Let's start with Leviticus 19:31: "Do not turn to mediums or seek out spiritists, for you will be defiled by them. I am the Lord your God." That is a key thought about witchcraft – *it will defile you*. The Hebrew word here for "defiled" could also be translated "contaminated" or "polluted." This Hebrew word appears 84 times in Leviticus alone, and it's usually translated "unclean." You find it especially in those chapters involving "unclean" foods or animals, and the "uncleanness" of those with "leprosy." Involvement with witchcraft makes you a spiritual leper. You are unclean and defiled.

Don't seek after "spiritists." Some translations use "wizards" or "fortune-tellers." Again, no Christian should ever have to consult a spiritist when he has the Holy Spirit! Why consult someone who is spiritually dead when you can talk to the Living One! Remember the words of the prophet in Isaiah 8:19-20: "When they say to you, 'Seek those who are mediums and wizards, who whisper and mutter,' should not a people seek their God? Should they seek the dead on behalf of the living? To the law and to the testimony! If

---

[46] See Leviticus 11:44-45, 19:2, 20:26, and 21:8. See also how it is quoted in 1 Peter 1:16.
[47] See Romans 3:20.

they do not speak according to this word, it is because there is no light in them." Seek God. Go to the Word of God.

I really like this phrase at the end of the verse – "I am the Lord your God." It appears over and over again in the Law of God. Basically, obey what I'm telling you in Leviticus 19:31 because I said so! I'm the Lord, that's why you need to obey this instruction. Your Master is telling you not to do this, so obey what He says!

I remember many times my kids asked me, "Dad, why do we need to do this or that?" I would respond, "Because I'm your dad, that's why!" The Lord is saying – Just do it. I know what is right. I said so and that's enough. No further explanations are needed.

Leviticus 20:6 has an even stronger word – "I will set My face against the person who turns to mediums and spiritists to prostitute himself by following them, and I will cut him off from his people." That is scary language: "God sets His face against the person." He is personally going to oppose someone to his face. This is a divine confrontation, and any person who comes face to face with God is going to lose.

Notice the language now – "to prostitute himself." The NLT reads, "Who commit spiritual prostitution by putting their trust in mediums." The KJV uses, "To go a whoring after them." It is an act of spiritual adultery and prostitution to consult a practitioner of the occult. You become a spiritual whore. It's like you've taken off with another lover. You're in bed having sex with someone else. This is an act of betrayal and treachery against God Himself. God will not tolerate it. He will "cut off that person." In other words, he's going to die! The death penalty is for anyone who engages in witchcraft. This is what God thinks of "mediums" and "spiritists." They are servants of Satan and you must have nothing to do with them!

What the Lord requires from us is found in the next verse: "Consecrate yourselves and be holy, because I am the

Lord your God" (v7). Sanctify yourself. Set yourself apart. Be holy. Don't defile, pollute, or contaminate yourself with witchcraft. Why curse yourself with these dark people and their evil practices? The power of God is infinitely greater than the power of Satan. If you don't know something or don't understand what's happening with your life, seek God. Look to the Holy Spirit, the divine teacher, to guide you into all truth. Paul wrote, "For the Spirit searches all things, yes, the deep things of God. Even so no one knows the things of God except the Spirit of God."[48] *The only one who knows everything about God is the Spirit of God.* Why consult a spiritist when you can consult the Spirit?

Again, the verse concludes with "Because I am the Lord your God." Do it because of Me. I am your Lord. I am your God. I'm giving you instructions and commandments that will bless your life if you obey them. I said so, so do it!

The final verse I want to consider in Leviticus is the last verse of Chapter 20. Again, this chapter gives us the "penalty phase" of sins committed in Chapters 18 and 19. This verse reads, "A man or woman who is a medium or spiritist among you must be put to death. You are to stone them; their blood will be on their own heads." First of all, it doesn't matter whether they are male or female, the penalty is the same. There is no gender bias with God. Anyone who chooses to be an actual medium or spiritist *must be put to death*. This gives us all a strong indication of what God thinks about witchcraft. Then it adds the method of death – "You are to stone them." In our day, we use the electric chair or a lethal injection. Some countries use a firing squad. Years ago, our country used hangings to punish the worst offenders. The people who participated with John Wilkes Booth in the assassination of President Abraham Lincoln in

---

[48] See 1 Corinthians 2:10-11.

1865 were all hanged from a noose. In OT Israel, they stoned people to death.

What does it mean that "their blood will be on their own heads?" Some translations read, "they have brought it on themselves," "they are responsible for their own death," or "they have caused their own doom." In other words, they have been warned. If they suffer death, sickness, or calamity, it's their own fault. God is saying to all people, that if anyone practices witchcraft or is a practitioner of sorcery, God is going to oppose and resist him on every side. People have been warned, and if they continue on in sorcery, they are in willful disobedience to the clear commands of God. They themselves are responsible for the consequences.[49]

YouTube Video: **The Christian and Witchcraft 14**

---

[49] A few sentences in this paragraph were taken from my teaching, *The Homosexual Christian?* See page 4.

THE CHRISTIAN & WITCHCRAFT

15

Pornography and Violent Videos

Most men start viewing pornography at a very early age. Years ago, it was with printed magazines, but today, everyone has easy access to raunchy flesh through the Internet. At one-time, young boys began viewing it at the age of fourteen, then thirteen, now eleven, and some are reporting lower numbers like eight years of age. A Christian teenager told me recently that teens at his high school regularly meet in the school bathrooms to watch hard-core pornography on cell phones during school breaks.

I'll never forget the man whose father became very ill and was hospitalized. He was in intensive care for nearly ten days before he finally passed away.

This man asked if I would officiate the funeral. Of course, I agreed. Even though I didn't know his father very well, I knew him, the son. There were some hard feelings during the funeral because the father had gambled all of his life and he physically abused several people in the home, including his wife, for many years.

This father had also immersed his heart and soul in pornography. In fact, the son told me that there was about forty years of pornographic magazines and literature in that house. It was found everywhere – garage, closets, attic, and bedrooms. This son had to rent a large trash storage bin to haul away all of the pornography. He later told me that once all the pornography left that house, a suffocating heaviness was also removed from the "atmosphere" of that place. The dark cloud of pornography left and people there could "breathe again."

Pornography is an oppressive, harsh, cruel, and depressing influence in so many homes and lives today. Once a man or woman submits his spirit to such wicked material, they often remain in bondage for a lifetime. It is a terribly sad reality, that digital and photographic images of nude women (women whom these men will never touch) hold them captive – spirit, soul and body. Pornography defiles and enslaves like nothing else.

Another story comes to mind that involves pornography. When I first heard this lady describe what happened to her mother, I immediately concluded that it was demonic. Her brother, an adult, struck his own mother with a two by four across the face.

Years earlier, this man was involved in a car accident that caused him to change dramatically. He went into a deep depression and it opened the door to a demonic world of dark movies, worldly music, and wicked pornography. Suddenly, he was in and out of mental wards. He claimed that he was hearing voices that told him to hurt himself, his other sister, and his mother. One voice told him to strike his mother. I remember the Bible verses that say, "He who strikes his father or his mother shall surely be put to death" and "cursed is the one who treats his father or his mother with contempt."[50]

The man was arrested and went to jail. This sister, who attended our church, told me that there was something dark and oppressive about her brother's room. He lived at home with his mother and father. After she described the situation further, I agreed to go to her mother's house and pray over the room. As I prayed and reflected on what she told me, I asked her if I could bring a CD player and some praise and worship music. Of course, she consented.

We agreed to meet at the church parking lot, and then we headed to her mom's house which is about forty-five minutes southeast. Her husband accompanied us.

As we walked into the house, I noticed the man's room off to the right. The door was locked. The room was dark, the curtains drawn, and the air in that room had no circulation. The minute we walked in, it was difficult to breathe. There was an oppressive heaviness in the room. I was in good physical shape, but I actually felt pressure against my chest. I immediately noticed all the demonic and violent videos on the bookshelves. Some of the videos were the "cop killing" type. There were also lots of pornographic videos and his personal desktop computer was loaded with porn.

We found an electrical outlet for the CD player and inserted a praise and worship CD into it. We drew open the curtains to let in some light, and then for the next hour and thirty minutes, we worshipped God in spirit and in truth in that room. The more we worshipped, the more the heaviness left the room. We prayed against everything that was in that room.

Whenever that man entered his room and closed the door, he left the outside world and entered into his demonic world of perverted music, movies, and videos. He was

---

[50] See Exodus 21:15 and Deuteronomy 27:16.

oppressed and he wanted to oppress others. The violent videos got into his spirit and he became violent. He became just like the images he was watching. Twice the Psalmist writes about idols – "Those who make them will be like them, and so will all who trust in them."[51]

When we were done worshipping, we were all as light as a feather. All sense of heaviness was gone. I asked the lady to throw away all the dark videos that were in that room and burn them in the back (which they did). As long as he was in jail, there was no one to oppose the burning of his demonic paraphernalia.

If you are a person who owns pornography in any form – videos, movies (R or X-rated), magazines, pictures, or on computer – get rid of it now! Pornography curses and defiles your spiritual life. Repent, renounce, and burn. Over the next few weeks and months, pray that the Lord will deliver and cleanse your heart and mind from such perverse defilement. I also strongly recommend Merlin Carothers' book, *What's On Your Mind?* This book will help cleanse your thought life from sexually explicit thinking. Carothers uses "the washing of water by the Word" (Ephesians 5:25) to sanctify your spirit. May the power of the Holy Spirit wash your mind and make you pure.

YouTube Video: **The Christian and Witchcraft 15**

---

[51] See Psalm 115:8 and 135:18.

16

King Saul and the Witch at Endor

"Then Saul said to his servants, 'Find me a woman who is a medium, that I may go to her and inquire of her.' And his servants said to him, 'In fact, there is a woman who is a medium at En Dor.'"
(1 Samuel 28:7)

One of the strangest stories in the entire Bible is found in 1 Samuel 28. It is the story of when King Saul consulted a medium in the city of Endor. You can learn many spiritual lessons here.

Saul was very desperate. Everything was going wrong. He was surrounded on every side. People were dying. Nothing was working for him. He was on edge. Simply put, *what he was begging for was a word from God.* Interestingly, when God is silent, it shatters our peace.

Saul could not consult the prophet Samuel because he had just died (v3). He prayed for God to speak to him in

THE CHRISTIAN & WITCHCRAFT

a dream, but a dream never came (v6). He talked to some "prophets," but none of them had a word. He consulted the "Urim" and the Thummim, but nothing happened (v6). He couldn't go to "the mediums and spiritists" in the land, because King Saul himself had kicked out all of them from the land (v3 and v9).

The truth is that long ago, Saul had hardened his heart against the Lord. He had rejected the Lord and the Lord had rejected him. His kingdom was stripped away by God Himself. David was the God-anointed and God-appointed king. Saul would rather offer a sacrifice than be obedient to the Lord. Samuel gave him an ominous word that struck panic and fear in his very soul: "Behold, to obey is better than sacrifice...for rebellion is as the sin of witchcraft, and stubbornness is as iniquity and idolatry. Because you have rejected the word of the Lord, He also has rejected you from being king." No matter what he did from that point, Saul's kingdom was empty and void of all strength and power. He no longer had God's approval or support. He was a dead man walking.

The pressing issue was that the "Philistine army" was attacking the king and his army, and Saul was utterly terrified of what the barbaric Philistines would do (verses 4-5). The old saying is that "in desperate times, men do desperate things." In his moment of despair, he asked "his servants," "Find me a woman who is a medium, that I may go to her and inquire of her." They said, "There is a woman who is a medium at En Dor" (v7).

It's amazing what people (we) will do when we disobey God. Saul "disguised himself," "changed clothes," and "came to the woman at night" (v8). We can never be ourselves. We instantly become frauds and we deceive ourselves and others.

He told the witch, "Please conduct a séance for me, and bring up for me the one I shall name to you" (v8). She was a necromancer, because she apparently specialized in bringing up the dead. She asked, "Whom shall I bring up for you?" He said, "Bring up Samuel for me" (v11). He thought he could get a word from God through a dead prophet. When Samuel came up as "a spirit out of the earth," only the medium saw him, not Saul or his two men. Amazingly, Samuel still appeared as "an old man covered with a mantle." Samuel's appearance brought Saul to his knees. He "fell with his face to the ground and bowed down" (v14).

Samuel wanted to know why Saul was "disturbing him" (v15). Saul explained the distress caused by the presence of the Philistine army, and worse, because God was completely silent. Samuel reminded Saul in verse 16 – "So why do you ask me, seeing the Lord has departed from you and has become your enemy?" What fearful words! Not only is God not speaking, He is now your avowed enemy! He adds the worst words Saul could possibly hear: "For the Lord has torn the kingdom out of your hand and given it to your neighbor, David. Because you did not obey the voice of the Lord nor execute the fierce wrath upon Amalek, the Lord has done this thing to you this day. Moreover, the Lord will also deliver Israel with you into the hand of the Philistines, and tomorrow you and your sons will be with me. The Lord will also deliver the army of Israel into the hand of the Philistines" (verses 17-19). At this point, Saul collapsed and became "dreadfully afraid." He had no more physical or spiritual strength. He was completely running on empty. At the very core of his being, he was completely exhausted. He had nothing more left to offer himself, his family, or the nation of Israel. He was done!

In 1 Samuel 31, you see Saul's tragic end. He and his three sons were killed. He was actually wounded in battle and committed suicide later by falling on his sword. The Philistines beheaded him and nailed his body to the "wall of Beth Shan." Saul was gone and so was his kingdom.

Do I really need to say this to Christian people? *Never consult anyone who practices witchcraft. Never.*

Ever. No tarot cards. No Ouija boards. No horoscopes. No psychics, wizards, palm readers, or sorcerers. Anything and everything associated with witchcraft will bring a curse into your life. You are playing with fire and you will be burned. Demons are involved and they will put a terrible hook in your jaw that will hold you captive for many years to come. Go to Jesus Christ. Go to the Word of God. Go to the light, not the darkness!

May the God of peace deliver us from every evil influence of sorcery and witchcraft. The Lord is mighty to deliver us from the evil one. Lord, lead us not into temptation, but deliver us from the evil one. Amen.

<u>*YouTube Video*</u>: **The Christian and Witchcraft 16**

17

Evil Objects, Books, Artifacts, and Symbols

*"He removed Maachah, the mother of Asa the
king, from being queen mother, because she had
made an obscene image of Asherah; and Asa cut
down her obscene image, then crushed and
burned it by the Brook Kidron."*
(2 Chronicles 15:16)
*"Josiah put away those who consulted mediums
and spiritists, the household gods and idols, all
the abominations that were seen in the land of
Judah and in Jerusalem."*
(2 Kings 23:24)

If you really want to get rid of something, you
need to burn and destroy it. Fire gets rid of things
permanently.

This is what the Lord told His people to do in the Old
Testament with all of the altars, idols, and images of the
pagan nations. This verse is representative of so many that
you find: "You shall destroy their altars, and break down

their sacred pillars, and cut down their wooden images, and burn their carved images with fire."[52] These are the words you find over and over again – "destroy," "break down," "cut down" and "burn with fire." In other words, completely annihilate, demolish, obliterate, and wipe out anything that will ensnare your soul and take you away from Me (the Lord).

We see above the godly kings, Asa and Josiah, throwing down and burning the objects of idolatry and witchcraft among God's people. Asa "cut down," "crushed," and "burned" the graven image that his mother made. Josiah threw down all the servants of Satan in the land. In those early years, these two men were serious about obeying God's Word.

When Paul got to Ephesus in Acts 19 – a city dominated by witchcraft, idolatry, and demonic activity – he commanded the new believers to publicly burn their scrolls of sorcery and magic (vv 18-20). The incredible value of these scrolls, 50,000 drachmas, did not hinder them. This would be worth millions of dollars today. They could have sold these items and made a lot of money, but why pass on the curse to someone else? When the element of witchcraft was removed from that area, "the word of the Lord spread widely and grew in power." A revival broke out. This is commonly reported in countries where witchcraft is a central part of the life of a society.

For many, many years now, I have witnessed multitudes of people who have demonic objects, books, artifacts, and symbols in their possession. Many of these items are innocently stored in a closet, garage, bookcase, or shelf somewhere. Little do people know that these items bring unforeseen curses into their lives.

In this final chapter, I want to give you a fairly comprehensive list of items that bring curses and even

---

[52] See Deuteronomy 7:5.

demonic activity into people's lives and homes. Along the way, I want to quote from various passages of the Bible that exhort people to burn this ungodly paraphernalia.

Moses had to challenge the sorcerers of Egypt; Daniel lived among occult practitioners in Babylon; the children of Israel were nearly destroyed by the seduction introduced by Balaam the soothsayer who was gifted in divination; King Saul consulted a witch at Endor; Josiah had to remove the mediums, sorcerers, and all the witchcraft introduced by other kings in Judah; Peter rebuked Simon the sorcerer in Samaria; Paul cursed Elymas the sorcerer with blindness at Paphos; Paul also had to cast out a "spirit of divination" (python) from a slave girl at Philippi; and scrolls of sorcery were burned in Ephesus. Galatians teaches that "witchcraft" or "sorcery" is a work of the flesh; Samuel said that "rebellion is as the sin of witchcraft."[53] Revelation shows that "sorcerers" are cast into the lake of fire, and they are included with "dogs,"[54] "murderers," "liars," and the "sexually immoral" outside the city of God. Yes, witchcraft is mentioned a lot in the Bible.

Let's look at different items that you may own that need to be destroyed or "burned in the fire." We'll start with some books.

Books Promoting the Cults

One of the most popular and accepted cult groups are the Mormons or the Church of Jesus Christ of Latter-Day Saints. They are headquartered in Salt Lake City, Utah, the Mormon capital of the world. Besides using the Bible, they also have books that they consider inspired including *The Book of Mormon*, *The Book of Doctrine and Covenants*, and

---

[53] See Galatians 5:20 and 1 Samuel 15:23.
[54] The "dogs" here, like those in Philippians 3:2, are referring to unclean people, not animals. The sorcerers are mentioned in Revelation 21:8 and 22:15. See also 9:21 and 18:23.

The Pearl of Great Price. If you have these three "extra" books, throw them in the trash or burn them with fire. Don't take them to a bookstore and get money for them. Why pass on the curse to other people?

Another common cult group that is full of false and heretical teachings is the Jehovah's Witnesses (JW's)[55] headquartered in Brooklyn, New York (now Warwick). They have their own version of the Bible – *The New World Translation* – which is completely corrupt. This book must be burned. JW's regularly leave *Watchtower* magazines, tracts, and other literature at my door. These items are quickly ripped up and thrown into the trashcan.

Mary Baker Eddy (1821-1901) founded the false group, Church of Christ, Scientist. She wrote a book entitled *Science and Health with Key to the Scriptures.* There is no need to detail all the false concepts and beliefs found in this book. Let it be burned.

In 1954, L. Ron Hubbard (1911-1986) founded the Church of Scientology. In 1950, he wrote the now famous, *Dianetics: The Modern Science of Mental Health.* In this book, Hubbard claims that he has found a technique to achieving better mental health by confronting memories that are not available to the conscious mind. His "church" following has spread to 140 countries and over eight million adherents. Hollywood has a massive church dedicated to his corrupt beliefs, and many famous actors and actresses are Scientologists. *Dianetics* is a worthless book that must be removed and destroyed.

Herbert Armstrong (1911-1986) founded the Worldwide Church of God. He also started Ambassador College in Pasadena. He rejected the Trinity as a satanic

---

[55] See my video teachings on YouTube or our website, teacherofthebible.com, or my book all entitled, *Witnessing to Jehovah's Witnesses.*

counterfeit and taught British Israelism. He also believed in a form of Sabbatarian doctrine and had many other false and heretical teachings. Any of his teachings or books must be thrown away.

There are many other cult groups that preach a "different gospel." You can consult books like *The Kingdom of the Cults* by Walter Martin and determine whether a church or group is truly of God.

Books Promoting Demonic Themes or Eastern Mysticism

At the time of this writing the *Harry Potter* series of books have sold nearly 600 million copies worldwide, making it the most popular series in history. These books, and now films, promote wholesale witchcraft to  young and old alike. It is one of the subtlest ways that Satan has invaded the hearts and minds of our young people.

In 1998, our local school district gave a hardback copy of the latest book to every student and teacher in the district. Hundreds of thousands of dollars were spent on books filled with witchcraft. The school district innocently said that they wanted to encourage reading among elementary-aged children. It is interesting subject material that will keep the kids engaged, they said. I promptly took my wife's copy (she was a kindergarten teacher) and burned it in a bonfire in my backyard with my young daughter present. I wanted her to see what we thought of witchcraft.

The *Koran* – and any books touting the virtues of Islam – should be burned in the fire. Because of the fear of revenge and terrorism, most people, including governments, are afraid to say anything against the Muslims and their "holy" book. Yet it is from its very sayings that jihadists worldwide are inspired to kill others for the glory of Allah.

Any books on astrology or reincarnation are false. Anton LaVey (1930-1997) was the founder of the Church of Satan and author of several books including *The Satanic Bible*, *The Satanic Rituals*, *The Satanic Witch*, *The Devil's Notebook*, and *Satan Speaks!* Obviously, this is demonic stuff and must be destroyed. Along this line, any books or materials involving black magic, sorcery, witch's brew, and candle lighting should be trashed or destroyed. I was amazed many years ago when I worked with a very intelligent computer programmer who had an entire collection of "witch" books with recipes and brews that could be concocted.

There are many books and materials which promote I Ching, Yin & Yang, Tai Chi, and yoga. I know Christians who practice yoga on a daily basis. This is a totally false and worldly practice. Anything that promotes Shamanism, Hinduism, Buddhism, Taoism, and Transcendental Meditation is demonic. In our area, we have many Hmong who live their lives governed by the local shaman (a witch doctor). All of this must be categorically rejected.

When I was in college, the books of Edgar Cayce (1877-1945) the self-professed clairvoyant, Carlos Castañeda (1925-1998) a promoter of shamanism, and Jeane Dixon (1904-1997) an American astrologer and psychic were very popular. Today, we have self-help authors like Wayne Dyer (1940-2015), who appears to innocently promote his brand of successful living. Dyer's *Your Erroneous Zones* has sold nearly 35 million copies. What a total waste of people's money!

Nostradamus was a 16th Century French physician who made several famous prophecies that supposedly have come true. There's no need to read his false predictions.

As I mentioned in Chapter 13, any Halloween stuff including demonic masks, outfits for witches, skeletons, creepy clowns, zombie stuff, grim reaper materials, and anything that promotes this satanic day must be destroyed.

Many years ago, I made the serious mistake of going on a school field trip with my young daughter to the Rosicrucian Egyptian Museum in San Jose, California. This museum, which claims to have the most artifacts of Ancient Egypt in the United States, was founded by the Ancient Mystical Order Rosae Crucis. Rosicrucianism was a 17th and 18th century movement professing esoteric and occult wisdom with emphasis on mysticism and spiritual enlightenment. Nothing associated with Ancient Egypt and Rosicrucianism is of the Lord.

Books and Artifacts Promoting Ancient and Modern Indian Spirituality

The Aztecs occupied a region of what is now southern Mexico and Guatemala back in the 1400s. Their capital was Tenochtitlan (present-day Mexico City). Hernan Cortes and the Spaniards destroyed this empire from 1519-1521. The Aztecs were given to idolatrous worship and human sacrifices. The Toltecs, or literally "the people from Tollan," dominated central and southern Mexico prior to the Aztecs in the 10th Century. They build pyramid temples, the largest of which was dedicated to Quetzalcoatl, the Plumed Serpent, an ancient deity the Toltec adopted from earlier cultures and worshiped as the god of Venus. The Mayan civilization dominated southern Mexico (the Yucatan Peninsula), Guatemala, Belize, and El Salvador from 300 to 900 AD. They worshipped various sky, maize, rain, and rainbow deities. Their idolatry included the worship of Ixtab, the goddess of suicide, and they believed that those who committed suicide went to a special heaven. Like the

Aztecs, the Mayans were involved with various forms of human sacrifice.

Many tourists innocently go to visit the ancient ruins left by these idolaters and buy replicas of their gods and goddesses or purchase artifacts that tout the virtues of these civilizations. My wife and I recently vacationed in Cancun, Mexico and toured the ruins at Tulum. There were busloads of tourists buying many replicas (cursed objects) of artifacts as souvenirs. Don't bring these items into your house nor accept them as gifts from friends!

A few years ago, we visited the Grand Canyon National Park in northern Arizona. We stayed in a hotel just east of the park near the large Hopi Reservation. Of course, it seemed that the towns in and around this reservation were filled with small museums and gift shops touting the virtues of these idolatrous people. Many of the Indian jewelry pieces that so many love to wear have had curses pronounced over them by these native Indian tribes. Also, as we mentioned in Chapter 11, dream catchers have their origins from the Native American Indian people. Christians must burn and destroy any Indian paraphernalia.

Magazines, Cards, and Games

Tarot card readings are a form of divination. These cards are a set of usually 78 playing cards, including 22 pictorial cards, used for fortune-telling. Several people in our church, before they became Christians, played Ouija boards. Some told me that supernatural events began happening around them while playing the board including objects moving with no one touching them. The Ouija board is also known as a "spirit board" or "talking board" because through questions and answers, people seek telepathic messages. Tarot cards and Ouija boards are clearly demonic. These occult items must be burned in the fire.

When I was in college back in the late 1970s, a new role-playing game was all the craze at UCLA where I attended. It was called Dungeons and Dragons. Many of my fellow engineers and scientists in my fraternity would stay up all night and weekends playing this demonic game. Since 1997, this game has been published by Wizards of the Coast, and you can role-play in stories like *Rage of Demons, Curse of Strahd, Elemental Evil,* and *Tyranny of Dragons.* Their website opens with the picture of a demon with murderous eyes and two large horns. Don't play Dungeons and Dragons!

I am familiar with the bondage of pornography. It defiles. It perverts. It corrupts.

One day, when I was eleven years old, I rode my bicycle to a local gas station about one city block from my house. I went there often to buy candy. Next to the gas station was a truck stop area lined with large shade trees. I rode my bike over by the trees to stay out of the hot desert sun for a few minutes. I noticed that a *Penthouse* magazine was thrown next to one of the trees by one of the truck drivers. I didn't know what a porn magazine was at that point in my life. I was innocent. But my innocence was scattered when I saw a picture of nearly naked woman on the front cover. My eyes were immediately riveted to her body. As I looked through that magazine over the next few hours, a spirit of lust came upon me. I took that magazine home and hid it under my bed. It was terrible. From that moment until I met Christ Jesus at the age of 22, I did not see women innocently again. I weep even today that the Lord had mercy on me and delivered me from that great darkness.

No one is absolutely sure of the exact statistics, but estimates from reputable monitoring agencies say that between 33% and 50% of all traffic on the Internet is pornographic. Some recent medical and Christian studies even indicate that pornography alters the chemistry of your physical brain. Malcolm Muggeridge (1903-1990), the well-known English journalist and satirist, once asked the question, "How do I know that pornography defiles?" His simple answer was "I know it defiles because it has defiled me." He had personally tasted the perverted dregs of this poison of the soul. If you have anything pornographic in your house – magazines, pictures, movies, or digital images – destroy them now. If you don't destroy them, they will destroy you!

When I first became pastor of our church, after a time of prayer and fasting, the Lord revealed to me that a few of our members were reading the daily horoscopes in the local newspapers. I preached a simple message about consulting the Word of God instead of demonic sources. The word, "horoscope," is a Greek compound word. "Hōra" (time, hour) + "skopos" (watcher, observer). Literally, it is a "time watcher." One dictionary defines it as "an astrologer's description of the personality and future of a person based on the position of the planets in relation to the sign of the zodiac under which the person was born." Wow, that sounds complicated. If you need to know something about your future, why don't you talk to the blessed Holy Spirit. John 16:13 says, "He will show you things to come." The future is in God's hands. Put your faith and trust in Him.

A few years ago, a couple from our church went to the local fair. They went to see a show with a hypnotist. The hypnotist was actually "casting spells" and inducing people in a state of hypnosis. The hypnotist asked for volunteers from the audience. The wife refused to volunteer herself, but her gullible husband foolishly went forward. His wife told him later that he made a complete fool of himself in front of many people. Also, this man later told me that he felt different about his spiritual life. "Something was missing," he said.

I remember in high school, during a school assembly, the office staff invited a hypnotist to cast his spells and put people under through hypnosis. This hypnotist actually made several students (male) put on female clothing and wigs. They made complete fools of themselves.

There are several best-selling books on hypnotism with subtitles like *Dark Psychology, Covert Manipulation, Brainwashing,* and *Mind Control.* None of this is good.

Never go see a hypnotist nor volunteer yourself at a show. Paul said, "For as many as are led by the Spirit of God, these are sons of God" and "if you are led by the Spirit, you are not under the law." Jesus said, "When He, the Spirit of truth has come, He will guide you into all truth."[56] This may sound too simple, but the only guide we need is the Holy Spirit and the Word of God.

Occult Symbols and Objects

Revelation 12:9 and 20:2 read, "So the great dragon was cast out, that serpent of old, called the Devil and Satan, who deceives the whole world; he was cast to the earth, and his angels were cast out with him" and "the dragon, that serpent of old, who is the Devil and Satan." In Revelation 12:13-17, the "dragon" (v13) turns into a "serpent" (v14, v15) and then back to a "dragon" (v17). Dragons and serpents have long represented the devil.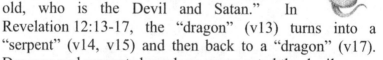

I remember more than twenty-five years ago, a young believer in the Lord who was on fire for the things of God was seduced sexually by a woman and caused him to turn away from God. When I went over to her house to deal with the situation, I noticed that the walls of her kitchen and family room were plastered with pictures and drawings of snakes, including cobras. I felt a demonic presence when I walked into that house.

Frogs and goats have also been used as demonic symbols. In 1972, before I knew Christ, I went to see the

---

[56] See Romans 8:14; Galatians 5:18; John 16:13.

horror classic, *Frogs*. I don't think I slept well for several weeks. It scared me half to death. Moses and Aaron confronted sorcerers in Egypt when they went to set God's people free. Exodus 8:2 says, "And the magicians did so with their enchantments, and brought up frogs on the land of Egypt."

In Matthew 25, Jesus separates "the sheep from the goats." The goats are placed at His left hand. Verse 41 says, "Depart from Me, you cursed, into the everlasting fire prepared for the devil and his angels." Before I was a Christian, I owned a famous music album that had goat heads on the cover and referenced the goats of Matthew 25. The music was demonic, and the singers and song writers of the album had devoted their lives to the devil and his work.

Think of all the things people bring home – Buddha figures, crystals, charms, amulets, fraternal rings, fetishes, crystal balls, rabbit's feet, prayer wheels, beads, and even neo-Nazi items and swastikas.

Music, Videos, and Digital Media

Today, there is so much demonic stuff entering our homes through music and movies. There are so many movies that promote witchcraft, wizards, and sorcery. Most of the popular movies today have some form of nudity or sexual language. Lots of movies blaspheme the name of the Lord. Many Disney movies have witchcraft – everything from *Fantasia* to *Snow White*, from the *Little Mermaid* to *Aladdin*.

The one area that gets in to our home the easiest is music. At the temptation of Christ in Matthew 4, we understand that Satan wants to be worshipped. He raises up people, makes them famous, so others can glorify him. There are many musicians who glorify the homosexual lifestyle – Freddie Mercury & Queen, Elton John, Village People, Boy George, Liberace, and Barry Manilow.

Manilow was married to a woman back in the 1960s, but he fell in love with Garry Kief, whom he has been with for over forty years now and married in 2014. When the Village People sang about the "YMCA" and being "in the Navy," that was the focus at the time for where homosexuals would act out or infiltrate. Freddie Mercury, who died of AIDS, wrote the song, *We Are the Champions*, to say that homosexuals would eventually conquer the world. The lyrics say:

> // We are the champions, my friends //
> // And we'll keep on fighting 'til the end //
> // We are the champions //
> // We are the champions //

Many people, including Christians, have music from the Eagles, Beatles, Alice Cooper, Marilyn Manson, AC/DC, Jerry Garcia and the Grateful Dead, Earth, Wind & Fire, Grand Funk, Led Zeppelin, and Rammstein. Many years ago, while a student in college, I attended an Earth, Wind, & Fire concert at the Long Beach Sports Arena. Maurice White (1941-2016), the band's leader and founder, began the concert by coming down from the rafters on a gold-colored pyramid as he pronounced curses on the audience.

In recent years, I have made numerous missionary trips to the island nation of Jamaica in the West Indies. I did a lot of study of the people and nation before I made my first trip in 2012. It was there that I came face to face with Rastafarianism. This cultic sect was founded in the 1930's and its adherents are known as Rastas. This mystical group became more popular with the rise of Bob Marley (1945-1981) and the Wailers. Marley made smoking marijuana a national pastime in Jamaica. Tragically, he died at the young age of 36 from melanoma. He was said to have fathered about thirteen children from ten different women. He almost single-handedly made reggae music one of the most popular music styles for several decades. He was a corrupter of a generation of young people in Jamaica. All Christians should burn any of his paraphernalia.

There are so many movies available on the popular market that glorify violence, suicide, cop killing, vampires/bats and sexual perversion. Movies like *Night of the Living Dead, Psycho* movies, *Texas Chainsaw Massacre, Exorcist, Rosemary's Baby, Shining, Willard, Carrie, Poltergeist, Halloween*, and *Alien* are dark and glorify the devil. I cannot tell you how many times I've walked into the homes of professing Christians who still have many of these movies in their personal library.

Catholic Mysticism & Statues

At this point, I must talk to my Catholic friends. Let me say this right up front – *No Christian believer needs any image, statue, candle, or object to have a personal relationship with the Lord Jesus Christ!* The simple fact is this: Jesus is alive; these objects are dead and lifeless.

You need to understand that I was born into a Catholic family. I went to a mass nearly every Sunday the first eighteen years of my life. I was baptized as an infant. I did my Holy Confirmation and First Holy Communion. I attended Catholic classes after school. I even ushered from time to time. I went to the confessions when I sensed the need. I was offered a full scholarship to Loyola Marymount University (a Jesuit school) to become a priest. While I wasn't living a godly life, nevertheless, I would never deny that I was a Catholic believer.

Catholics have lots of statues, candles, rosaries, and pictures of various mystical figures or saints. They have statues of the Virgin Mary, the Virgin de Guadalupe, and Our Lady of Lourdes. They have pictures of Papa Pio[57] on the walls of their home (as if his picture will somehow protect the home or bless it). Catholics, especially in Mexico, attend the Day of the Dead (Día de los Muertos) at cemeteries. They pray to the  saints and light candles. They burn incense. They say the "Hail Mary" prayer and try to get to Jesus "through the heart of Mary." They proclaim and believe the infallibility of the Pope. They believe the Pope is Christ's vicar[58] on earth.

Let me say it again: You don't need any image, statue, candle, or object to have a personal relationship with Jesus. Jesus is alive; statues are lifeless images. With all boldness, I say that you must take all of this Catholic paraphernalia and throw it away! Burn it! Do what Moses, Gideon, Asa, Josiah, Jehoiada and the early believers in Acts did – they destroyed and burned such items. They bring curses into your life. I'll go even further – *God hates these things*. It's a stumbling block to your relationship with Christ.

Nowhere in the Bible are we told to pray to a dead human being. Nowhere in the Bible are we told to pray to the Virgin Mary. The Bible specifically condemns the making of any images or statues. Right after the incident with the golden calf, Exodus 34:13-14 reads, "But you shall destroy their altars, break their sacred pillars, and cut down their wooden images (for you shall worship no other god, for the Lord, whose name is Jealous, is a jealous God)." In the

---

[57] Papa Pio (1887-1968) was a famous Italian priest, stigmatist, and mystic. He supposedly had the stigmata on his hands (like the nail prints on Jesus). In the Catholic Church, he is venerated as a saint.
[58] Basically, Catholics believe that the Pope acts as the personal substitute or representative of Christ here on earth.

Ten Commandments, God says, "You shall not make for yourself a carved image – any likeness of anything that is in heaven above, or that is in the earth beneath, or that is in the water under the earth; you shall not bow down to them nor serve them. For I, the Lord your God, am a jealous God."[59] Idolatry provokes the jealousy of God. This is very dangerous. Any images and statues of Catholic saints or the Virgin Mary that are used for prayer, lighting candles, or as some kind of protection to ward off evil are idolatrous. In the front of many, many houses in our city, there are such statues placed that help identify Catholic households. Truthfully, such images and statues draw people away from the true and living God.

The apostle John warned us at the end of his epistle: "Little children, keep yourselves from idols." He also commanded in Revelation, that we "should not worship demons, and idols of gold, silver, brass, stone, and wood, which can neither see nor hear nor walk." Paul told the young believers in Thessalonica, "How you turned to God from idols to serve the living and true God."[60]

The classic biblical statement against idols is found in Psalms 115:4-8. These verses apply directly to the images and statues found in Catholic churches and Catholic homes: "Their idols are silver and gold, the work of men's hands. They have mouths, but they do not speak; eyes they have, but they do not see; they have ears, but they do not hear; noses they have, but they do not smell; they have hands, but they do not handle; feet they have, but they do not walk; nor do they mutter through their throat. Those who make them are like them; so is everyone who trusts in them." That's the point – it was made by man. There is no life in them. They can't do anything but curse your life. We also become

---

[59] See Deuteronomy 5:8-9.
[60] The verses in this paragraph include 1 John 5:21; Revelation 9:20; and 1 Thessalonians 1:9.

lifeless when we somehow venerate or pray to such images that are made by human hands.

Sorcerers, Mediums, & Necromancers

Okay, I've said enough about all these items of witchcraft. It's time to draw to a close. Let me end with obvious servants of Satan. These are people who are clearly practicing witchcraft.

Let me start with Walter Mercado (1932-2019). Mercado was a Puerto Rican astrologer who was known by his stage name of Shanti Ananda. At the height of his popularity, this admitted homosexual was watched by over 120 million Latinos throughout Central and South America. He dressed flamboyantly (like Liberace) and read horoscopes in an intense and dramatic fashion. Without exaggeration, this man wore so much make-up that his face looked like that of a circus clown. In many ways, his face resembled the Joker of the Batman series. Mercado was very popular, but he was clearly a servant of Satan.

Years ago, a Christian couple came to our church with their four children. In a brief conversation at their house, I began talking to them about the dangers of witchcraft. I just happened to mention The Long Island Medium, Theresa Caputo. This Christian family told me that the show that featured Caputo was their favorite TV program! I was shocked. They were shocked when I told them that she was an instrument of Satan used to deceive people.

Caputo was trained by a lady named Pat Longo. Let me just write what you can find on Longo's website. "My name is Pat Longo and I have been blessed with the extraordinary ability to heal others by using the power of Divine energy. For over 20 years I have had the privilege of being instrumental in the miraculous healings of countless men, women, and children. I have been given the capability to channel Universal Energy with pure light and love through my hands to restore, correct, and transform energetic imbalances within my client's energy fields." I know people laugh at or mock such statements, but why do millions of gullible people watch such people? Caputo is booked up years in advance to do readings at her shows.

I've said this before and I'll say it again: *If you need a word from God, get into the Word of God.* The Lord will clearly speak to your heart if you begin to read and study His Word diligently. Don't be deceived by these people who practice witchcraft.

YouTube Video: **The Christian and Witchcraft 17**

THE CHRISTIAN & WITCHCRAFT

Chapter 1 – Study Questions

In the story of Tamika and Rosie the Spiritual Guide, why would someone as educated as Tamika seek help from a psychic?

Tamika was brought up in a Christian home. Why would she seek help for depression and anxiety from a psychic rather than from the Lord?

Chapter 2 – Study Questions

Read the story of Simon the sorcerer in Acts 8:9-24. In your own words, describe who he was and what he did:

Many Christians do not believe the Simon was truly saved. But he was baptized by Philip the evangelist, and Acts 8:13 seems to indicate that he was a believer. Do you think that Simon truly became a Christian? Why or why not?

Why did Peter tell Simon, "…and pray to God *if perhaps* the thought of your heart may be forgiven" (8:22)? Why should there be doubt about God's forgiveness of sins?

Chapter 3 – Study Questions

In the story of The Wizard of Indiana, how could Tom the wizard know all the details of Linda's life? How could a servant of Satan know such things?

God gave Pharaoh a dream that was interpreted by Joseph; God gave Nebuchadnezzar a dream that was interpreted by Daniel; and God gave Tom a dream that was interpreted by Barbara. Why does God sometimes use dreams to accomplish His purposes?

Chapter 4 – Study Questions

Read the story of Elymas in Acts 13:6-12. Who was he and what did he try to do?

Why did the apostle Paul curse Elymas with blindness? Why didn't he just try to tell him about Jesus and seek to win him to the Lord?

Chapter 5 – Study Questions

In Women and the Psychic Connection, why do you think that all palm readers and nationally syndicated astrologers are all women?

On page 32, Pastor Charlie makes the comment that "witchcraft is marriage breaker Number #1." Why do you think this is so?

Chapter 6 – Study Questions

Read Acts 16:16-19. In your own words, what happened in the encounter between the apostle Paul and the fortune-telling slave girl?

From this story in Acts 16, how can we know that all fortune-tellers are guided by evil spirits and they are merely out to make money or "a profit?"

Paul and Silas were severely persecuted for this supernatural deliverance of the slave girl. How did the Lord turn this evil into good with the salvation of the Philippian jailer and his family?

Chapter 7 – Study Questions

Read the story of the sorcery/magic scrolls that were burned in Acts 19:17-20. Why didn't these believers just sell these scrolls and make a lot of money for themselves or donate the money to the church?

How is it that immediately after these sorcery scrolls were burned that "the word of the Lord grew mightily and prevailed" (19:20)?

What was the connection between the problems in Derek Prince's ministry and the Chinese dragons in his home?

Chapter 8 – Study Questions

Do you think that drug addiction and drug dealing are forms of witchcraft? (Recall that the word for "sorcery" in Galatians 5:20 is pharmakeia.)

What does it mean in practical terms that the great city of Babylon "deceives all nations by its sorcery"? (Revelation 18)

Chapter 9 – Study Questions

Exactly how is it that a porcelain Buddha brought into a home or work cubicle can make someone sick?

Chapter 10 – Study Questions

Meditate on Deuteronomy 7:25-26. In your own words, what truths jump out at you when you consider these verses?

Read the story of Achan and the children of Israel in Joshua Chapter 7. In your own words, describe how Achan brought a curse upon himself and all Israel.

Chapter 11 – Study Questions

When reading about the little girl and the dream catcher, what was something that stood out for you in this story? Why?

Review the Indian legend about dream catchers on pages 63-64. In your own words, what are dream catchers all about?

Chapter 12 – Study Questions

Explain why Israel was commanded to put to death anyone who was a witch (Exodus 22:18; Leviticus 20:27). Why such a harsh penalty?

Pastor Charlie writes in this chapter that "soothsayers, wizards, mediums, necromancers, spiritists, and sorcerers do not have any special abilities of their own. They are working directly with demons." Explain this statement.

Chapter 13 – Study Questions

Do you consider Halloween to be evil? Should Christians allow their children to go "trick or treat?" Why or why not? (You may want to do a little research in encyclopedias or on-line resources and learn more about this day.)

Exactly how did Barbara begin to have nightmares from all the horror movies that she was watching?

Chapter 14 – Study Questions

Pastor Charlie writes, "Involvement with witchcraft makes you a spiritual leper. You are unclean and defiled." Explain this statement.

When commenting on Leviticus 20:6 on page 79, the author makes the following observation: "It is an act of spiritual adultery and prostitution to consult a practitioner of the occult. You become a spiritual whore." What does this mean?

Chapter 15 – Study Questions

What were some of the spiritual dynamics of the man who struck his own mother with a two by four across the face?

The author makes the statement that "pornography defiles and enslaves like nothing else." Why is this true?

Chapter 16 – Study Questions

Read the story of King Saul and the witch at Endor in 1 Samuel 28. In your own words, explain why Saul had to consult a witch.

Exactly how did a dead man's spirit (Samuel) speak to King Saul? (1 Samuel 28:15-19)

Chapter 17 – Study Questions

Of all the items listed in the chapter on "Evil Objects, Books, Artifacts, and Symbols," explain your previous involvement with any of these evil things. How were you introduced to it? How did it affect your life?

Do you think it is acceptable in God's eyes to listen to music produced/sung by practicing homosexuals? What about the *Harry Potter* movies or the *Lord of the Rings* series? Why or why not?

What was the most important lesson you learned in this book?

About the Author

Charlie Avila is the Senior Pastor of Clovis Christian Center in Fresno, California. He is married to Irma and has two adult children – Leah (husband: Jose) and Daniel. Pastor Charlie is the Bible teacher of the Spirit of Wisdom and Revelation teaching newsletters and the principal teacher on the Teacher of the Bible website.

He is an instructor with the Fresno School of Mission and other ministry schools. He has spoken in conferences locally, nationally, and internationally. He teaches special seminars on various Bible subjects and verse by verse studies through Old Testament and New Testament books. He has written several books available on Amazon including *The Christian and Anger, The Christian and Homosexuality, The Christian and Hell, The Christian & Witchcraft, Detecting & Dealing with False Teachings, Healing the Sick, How to Become a Christian, The End Times, Making Disciples One on One, Having Sex with Your Boyfriend, Witnessing to Jehovah's Witnesses* and various commentaries on books of the Bible including Esther, 2 Peter, and Jude. He also has many books in Spanish by the same titles as the English versions.

He can be contacted at teacherofthebible@gmail.com or Clovis Christian Center, 3606 N. Fowler Ave, Fresno, CA 93727-1124.

The 17 short video teachings for each chapter of this book are available on YouTube. Just type "The Christian and Witchcraft Pastor Charlie Avila" on the search line or type "Teacher of the Bible" and subscribe. The videos are also available at www.teacherofthebible.com.

Scriptural Reference Index

Made in the USA
Las Vegas, NV
03 October 2023

78504352R00080